LIFE.PERFECTED.

LIFE.PERFECTED.

UNDERSTANDING HOW TO USE MONEY
TO LIVE THE LIFE OF YOUR DREAMS

RYAN HEATH
RYAN PETERSON

LIFE.PERFECTED.

Understanding How to Use Money to Live the Life of Your Dreams

ISBN   978-1-61961-872-5   *Hardcover*

978-1-61961-873-2   *Paperback*

978-1-61961-871-8   *Ebook*

LIONCREST
PUBLISHING

To JFP, the original "Wizard of wealth."

CONTENTS

INTRODUCTION...9

1. IT'S NOT ABOUT THE MONEY 25

2. LAY YOUR FINANCIAL FOUNDATION...................... 49

3. INCOME PLANNING 77

4. INVESTING 115

5. TAXES... 137

6. LEGACY PLANNING... 153

7. TAKE ACTION 177

ACKNOWLEDGMENTS 191

ABOUT THE AUTHORS 195

INTRODUCTION

*Money is a terrible master but
an excellent servant.*

P. T. BARNUM

If there's one truth we've learned during our nearly half century of combined years in the financial services industry, it's that the vast majority of people we meet have no idea how money really works.

We've watched countless people walk into our offices for the first time with a look of apprehension on their faces because the thought of talking about their finances makes them nervous. They're worried about the questions we're going to ask, or that we're going to review their investment statements and tell them they're doing everything wrong.

Like going to the doctor, visiting a financial professional evokes certain feelings in people that are anchored to experiences they've had. Sadly, a lot of those experiences are unpleasant, and therefore negative anchoring has become commonplace in our industry.

We like to flip these expectations on their head.

Within minutes of talking to us, the same people realize they have no reason to worry because, while we're interested in helping them with their finances, we're more concerned with how money impacts their life. Are they working for their money, or is their money working for them?

People aren't trained to think about money in this way. From an early age, we're taught to get good grades in school, go to college, find a job that pays well, and start saving for retirement. We slave away for forty years hoping to hit "retirement age" and enjoy our remaining days living off the money we pray doesn't run out before we die.

Is that any way to live? We don't think so.

We'd rather use our money to create perfect moments we can enjoy today, while at the same time planning for perfect moments we'll enjoy in the future.

We're willing to bet you feel the same way. If so, you picked the right book. We're going to teach you what you need to know about using your money to fuel your ideal lifestyle. Our simple, back-to-basics approach doesn't require extensive financial acumen. You just need a willingness to learn how to apply the principles we're going to share.

Before we go any further, allow us to introduce ourselves and explain why you should consider the advice and strategies we're going to talk about in this book.

MEET RYAN HEATH

Growing up, money was tight. My father was a minister, and my mother stayed home to raise the kids. I didn't talk finances with my parents, but my father's work in the ministry left me with a desire to help people.

I was only twenty-five when I became the youngest person in the history of my publicly traded company to be named division manager and oversee operations for a multistate area. It was exciting to see what money could do for hundreds of people, but I grew frustrated with the backward approach I saw.

I left to form my own independent firm in 2004 and began crafting a better approach to financial planning. In 2010, I merged my practice into a regional bank where I served as president of the bank's wealth management division until 2015. It was then that I left to team up with my longtime friend, Ryan Peterson, to transform the company that Dr. John Philips had founded in 1986, into Copperleaf Capital, the SEC-registered investment advisory firm we own and operate together. We do things differently by helping our clients grow their wealth for the primary purpose of living a better life.

My career path has led me to a place where I can travel and work remotely, whether that be from a beach or a summer Airbnb in Europe with my family. I can live my ideal life throughout the year, rather than in chunks when it's time for vacation. That's my version of Life.Perfected.

MEET RYAN PETERSON

My mother was a social worker, and my father was an elementary school principal, so education and caring for others was at the heart of our household. I knew early on that I wanted to follow their rewarding path while developing a more entrepreneurial career.

It was an interaction with my friend's dad in seventh grade that sparked my fascination with the life of a financial advisor. I envied his dynamic lifestyle and the fact he got to travel the country so much. I had no idea what financial advising was, but I knew I wanted to do it.

After a decade working with several of the largest financial services companies in the United States, I decided to use my financial expertise to make a greater impact on the world. I moved to Raleigh, North Carolina, in 2003 and connected with Dr. John Philips. His firm helped doctors and other closely held small business owners to not only change their lives but also *enjoy* their lives.

My wife is a physician, so I shared Dr. Philips's passion for helping entrepreneurs in the medical and dental fields. His firm was the perfect fit for me. We've never wavered from that approach in fifteen years and have expanded our reach to include closely held businesses in a variety of different industries.

In addition to helping others, I also have a passion for learning. I've earned an MBA and three professional designations: Certified Financial Planner (CFP®), Chartered Life Underwriter (CLU), and Chartered Financial Consultant (ChFC).

In 2016, Ryan H. and I were part of a team of six cofounders to launch AE Wealth Management, an institutional investment advisory firm that serves a national network of top financial advisors and their clients. In just over eighteen months, AE Wealth Management has grown from nothing to managing over $2 billion in assets, making it one of the fastest growing investment advisory start-ups in the country.

My Life.Perfected. has included moving my family to Napa Valley from Raleigh. I now enjoy the perks of living in wine country with my family, while also serving our amazing clients across the United States. Years ago, I never would've thought that Napa Valley would someday be my home, but as we'll discuss, our dreams can change into something better than we ever could've imagined if we're open to the possibilities.

A FOCUS ON ADDING VALUE TO THE WORLD

Aside from our complementary skill sets—and the same terrible sense of humor—working together appealed to us because we both seek to add value to the world through our work. Neither of us wakes up in the morning consumed with the idea of making money. Any monetary gain we experience is a direct result of the value we add to the lives of our clients.

RYAN PETERSON

In 1991, I was in my first year as a financial advisor, and my manager sent me to an all-day motivational speaker seminar. It sounds cliché, but Zig Ziglar said something on stage that changed my life. He told us we could have everything we wanted in life if we just helped enough people get what they wanted in their lives. I discovered that my purpose, whether I get paid or not, is to help people improve their lives in meaningful ways. He was right.

In our line of work, adding value to people's lives doesn't mean adding dollars to their bank accounts. Some of the wealthiest people we've worked with—those with a nine-figure net worth—were aimlessly chasing a number on a page. We helped them realize that life is measured in moments, not money.

Pursuing money at the expense of your ideal life does not add value to your life or the lives of others. You might think it does, but it doesn't. If you've seen the film *Wall Street: Money Never Sleeps*, you may recall the scene where Shia LaBeouf asks Josh Brolin what number he's chasing. Brolin pauses for a moment before responding with a smile, "More."

The pursuit of "more" can cause parents to lose relationships with their kids because they've sacrificed time with them while chasing a bigger fortune. "More" can create health problems brought on by stress, lack of sleep, and poor diet and exercise habits.

"More" can take away from your world rather than adding to it.

If we can help others accept this truth—that life isn't about the money—then we've done our jobs. No other mindset shift has the potential to add more value to a person's life.

THIS IS NOT ANOTHER BOOK ABOUT MONEY

Given our backgrounds, it would've been all too easy for us to write a straightforward money book that explains something rudimentary such as the difference between a traditional and a Roth IRA. The world already has enough of those books. We will cover basic financial concepts in these pages, but we avoid getting too deep in the weeds with our explanations.

We also saw little value in taking a lofty, new age approach to money. Of all the things in life that can bring enlightenment, we're certain that money isn't one of them.

Between those two extremes lies our mission with this

book: *we want to empower you to use your money to create the life you want to live.*

Our approach to financial planning is practical and has purpose. We've found that you may grow personally, along with your wealth, when you take our approach to heart.

LEARN THE RULES OF MONEY

Money doesn't come with a rule book, and too few people learn how it's supposed to be used. So, in this book, we'll look at the rules of money. When you learn the ins and outs of money and see how it can work for you, then you'll be able to use your wealth to support your Life.Perfected.

Most people have never considered this concept because learning how money works isn't typically taught in schools or at home. As a result, the rules of money might feel overwhelming, but worry not. We're going to walk you through this process of discovery step by step, until you feel confident in your knowledge of how money works.

Each chapter of this book covers one of the rules of money, including income planning, investing, taxes, and legacy planning. We also share action steps you can take once you've finished the book.

The lessons in these chapters create a framework to get your money working for you. So many people spend their whole lives working for money because they don't know any better, or, worse, they believe more wealth equals more happiness. As we'll see in chapter 1, the people whose lives are about the pursuit of wealth can end up empty and unfulfilled.

Money is merely the tool you'll use to build the life of your dreams. Once you come to grips with this truth, the wealth you create throughout your life can serve its true purpose.

CREATE LIFE.PERFECTED.

You'll find purpose in learning how money works when you define and create your Life.Perfected. When we use this term, most people assume we're referring to the "golden years" after age sixty-five, when they get to retire and enjoy the fruits of their labor.

We have a friend who's built his life around this notion.

Our friend's goal is to have $5.5 million by the time he's fifty-five years old. His catchphrase is "five point five by fifty-five." While we certainly believe in setting goals, an age and a number have to be attached to a concrete purpose. When our friend reaches $5.5 million by fifty-five, will it make him happy? Or will his new goal be "six by sixty"?

We believe our friend is operating with an outdated mindset. By setting a goal, he's on the right track, but he needs to find the "why" behind it.

Rather than focusing solely on the future and working around the clock, he should begin using his accumulated wealth to create perfect moments right now that improve the quality of his life. Nobody should wait until "retirement age" to begin living Life.Perfected.

By seeking to create perfect moments, you begin purposefully designing your life, rather than letting life happen to you. Nobody's life will ever be perfect all the time, but you can live your ideal life by creating perfect moments each day, whether it's going for a walk with your spouse or meditating in the morning.

The accumulation of perfect moments, not wealth, creates a Life.Perfected.

RYAN PETERSON

We were finishing the final edits of this book when the worst wildfires in California history swept through Napa Valley, forcing my family to evacuate to my sister-in-law's house in Minnesota. We'd just spent the first weekend in our home after a complete renovation, and now there was a real chance we might lose everything. As I sat at the breakfast table one morning, I asked my wife, "How ironic is it that I'm writing a book about Life. Perfected. while this is happening?" Her response was a great reminder for me: "That's why Life.Perfected. is so important. The stuff we may lose is not the stuff that matters."

We'll help you define your ideal life in chapter 1 and then lay a financial foundation in chapter 2 that is essential to understanding the rules of money.

Our goal is to discover your "why" and use it as the foundation for everything you're going to build. Your "why" is the desire at the heart of your ideal life, be it more time with family, better health, or the ability to travel the world. As you learn new rules in each chapter, they'll be implemented to further enable your Life.Perfected.

A SIMPLE APPROACH IS BEST

A Life.Perfected. is not achieved overnight. It takes hard

work, patience, and discipline to build the kind of wealth that supports the life you want. If you're looking for how to become an overnight millionaire, you've picked up the wrong book. However, we encourage you to keep reading anyway, because on these pages you'll find answers to questions you likely haven't even thought of yet.

Also, if you're looking for fancy investment schemes, we don't use them. Here's why: they seldom work.

As some of you may be painfully aware, the true mission of the financial industry is often to separate you from your money. Industry professionals do this by constantly pushing new investment opportunities on you and cashing in with fees and expenses whenever you take the plunge. We're sharing this dirty little secret from "backstage Wall Street" to illustrate why we feel a back-to-basics approach is the more reliable way to maximize your money.

People who are drawn to the get-rich-quick schemes found in best sellers would probably call our approach "boring" or "old-fashioned." They're right.

We're proud of the fact that our approach is boring and old-fashioned. In fact, we designed it that way. Do you know why? Because boring and old-fashioned work! The reason our approach can be called old-fashioned is because it's endured for decades, while other flash-in-the-pan investment schemes burned bright and then faded away quickly.

We weren't interested in writing that kind of book. What we're going to share in these pages is a simple, back-to-basics approach to growing your wealth that will endure long after we're both gone. It's not "sexy," but the simple strategies we're going to share have produced a life of total financial independence for many of our clients over the years.

We operate by the motto of our business partner at AE Wealth Management and best-selling author David Bach: "You need to have a boring investment portfolio so you can have an exciting life."

These rules of money will teach you how to create a predictable income flow that enables your Life.Perfected. Whatever that life looks like to you, you can't live it if you're focusing on creating wealth and chasing a new investment scheme every year.

To live your ideal life, you must first define what that is for you and then begin to pursue it. These two steps happen before the rules of money are implemented because the "why" behind financial planning is more important than the "how." Once you have a clear vision of the life you want to live, then you can begin putting your money to work for you.

We're eager to help you discover what Life.Perfected. means to you. If you're as ready as we are, let's dive into chapter 1 and begin this exciting process.

IT'S NOT ABOUT
THE MONEY

Wealth is the ability to fully experience life.

HENRY DAVID THOREAU

We know what you're thinking. The people who say, "It's not about the money," usually have zero financial concerns. They're already wealthy, or at least financially secure, so those words ring hollow for people who do have to worry about money.

While money is critical to building an ideal life, we'd argue that money is not the result you should be chasing. Life.Perfected. can help you in the pursuit of wealth that enables your ideal life, but if your reward is the money itself, your life may feel empty.

Some of our wealthiest clients have proven that money isn't everything. In fact, the wealthiest among us are sometimes the unhappiest. They're tormented with anxiety over losing their fortune, and they sacrifice relationships to chase the next big payday.

While you might not feel bad for them, we hope their stories illustrate the danger of making your life all about the accumulation and management of wealth.

WEALTHY PEOPLE AREN'T ALWAYS HAPPY

One of our clients is a woman in her seventies whose husband built a hugely successful business. Her spending was reasonable for someone with her wealth—about $200,000 annually—so she never had to think too much about how money works.

All that changed the day her husband died and she became responsible for managing their $18 million estate. She came to us by referral and sat in our office with tears in her eyes, terrified that she was going to run out of money and die penniless. We both knew that unless she developed some very expensive habits, not even her grandchildren would outlive that money.

We once met with a family who has a net worth of $100 million, which sounds amazing until you realize they are all slaves to their business. We remind them often that life isn't about running your business, but rather about enjoying things that are important to you. However, they struggle to step away from the daily grind and the constant pursuit of greater wealth.

While not one of our clients (yet), Dallas Cowboys owner Jerry Jones is a billionaire whose life many people would be happy to live. But along with his jet-setting lifestyle and world-famous sports franchise comes the dark side to wealth most people never consider.

A simple Google search shows you that Jones has high-profile lawsuits to deal with and millions in payroll he has to cover each week. He's constantly juggling cash on hand versus credit to make ends meet. He owns a jet, but he has to pay millions a year just to keep it operating.

Yes, Jerry Jones's life is glamorous, but it's also stressful.

We tend to idolize the lives of the rich and famous as lavish and carefree, yet when we peel back the layers, we often find individuals who are stressed beyond belief. The wealthy sometimes face health problems brought on by stress, they're strangers to their own families, and they're constantly dealing with freeloaders trying to get a piece of their wealth.

It's easy to say to yourself, "I won't be like that when I'm wealthy," but living out those words is difficult. Wealth creates a slew of unanticipated problems that can derail your plans if you don't confront them head on.

WEALTH CAN'T BUY A FEELING OF SECURITY

In addition to fear and worry, the feeling of security often tends to decrease the wealthier someone becomes. This sounds bizarre, but why else would a woman worth $18 million sit in our office crying at the thought of dying destitute? Why would a family worth $100 million work eighteen hours a day instead of using their wealth to live the life we all dream about—one free from financial worry?

Both clients demonstrate the primary reason we feel wealthy people can still be anxious: because they don't understand how money works, their wealth feels like a burden.

In our experience, the wealthy are either scared of spending what they have too quickly and running out of money, or they're worried about spending too slowly and missing out on good opportunities. When people can't evaluate how much money they'll need or know how fast they can spend, they miss the point of having wealth because they're so twisted up with worry.

When we have clients like this, our goal is to untangle them from the web of worry that's ensnared them. We do this by explaining that Life.Perfected. is about being free to live within your values, and while wealth can help you do that, money is not the result we should be chasing.

The reactions we get in that moment are what make our jobs so much fun. It's a total light bulb moment for people who have spent decades chasing every dollar or pinching pennies because they never knew how to assess their wealth or just never made that effort.

As we begin to help clients unpack the mechanics of money and discover what their ideal life looks like, that feeling of security typically returns. The fear that caused them to chase or hoard money no longer twists up their insides. For the first time, they stop using their life to serve the pursuit of money and start using their money to serve the pursuit of their life.

We help them discover a truth they've long ignored:

I can live a life of perfection right now.

Life.Perfected. is not about the money. It's about using money as a tool to do what you love. With that in mind, let's consider what it means to live a life of perfection and how you can discover what "perfection" means to you.

A SERIES OF PERFECT MOMENTS

Nobody's life will ever be perfect all the time. Money can't buy you happiness, nor can it help you escape pain. The ups and downs of life are all part of the human experience. The same is true with your finances. We didn't write *Life. Perfected.* to help you build a portfolio that never loses money—no book can do that.

An ideal life comes from creating and enjoying perfect moments. When you string these perfect moments together consistently, you'll enjoy Life.Perfected. No matter where you are in life or how much money you have, living a "perfect life" means seizing perfection every chance you get to create those moments of pure happiness.

RYAN PETERSON

My wife and I have made it a point to try to sprinkle in perfect moments throughout our day. We just finished a big home remodel, which was crazy and stressful at times. In the middle of those stressful moments, we'd pause and say, "Let's have a perfect moment right now and go for a walk to get some fresh air." While this might sound corny, we know that life gets in the way sometimes. If we don't make a conscious effort to schedule moments like these, they might not happen.

Perfect moments are often simple and inexpensive.

What we've found is that the majority of our clients don't want extravagant lifestyles, but rather, comfortable lives in which they can enjoy happiness with those they love. The only requirement of a perfect moment that we see is that it's meaningful and makes you happy. When you keep the requirements simple, you're more likely to create and enjoy perfect moments every day.

In this chapter, we'll help you discover what a perfect moment looks like for you, and how such moments can inform what the life of your dreams looks like. Before we get into that, let's touch on another point that's foundational to your understanding of this concept.

AN IDEAL LIFE LOOKS DIFFERENT TO EVERYONE

One of the reasons we use perfect moments as the building blocks of an ideal life is that moments are easier to conceptualize than giant, life-changing shifts. Focusing on moments also allows us to drill down and discover what Life.Perfected. means to each individual, which is a crucial step, because everyone's definition is different.

On the surface, almost everyone's definition of perfection is the same. Most of us want a greater feeling of security, more time with family, less stress, more fun experiences, and the peace that comes from knowing we've found what life's all about. In this book, we want to dig a little deeper and fill this basic blueprint in with moments that matter to you. Once we do that, you'll have a clear vision of the ideal life you want to pursue.

RYAN HEATH

My daughter loves golfing, so when I asked her what a perfect moment means to her, she told me simply that it's playing golf as a family at the club in our neighborhood and getting lunch afterward. I learned a lot from hearing what an eight-year-old wants most in this world: playing golf with her parents and having lunch together. As a dad, I love my daughter's answer, because I can give her perfection any day we choose.

In addition to family time, we've learned that moments of perfection can happen in business, such as when you deliver good news to a client. They can happen in charitable ways, when you donate money or help those in need. You can also experience them in moments of solitude, when you do something perfect for yourself. It's safe to say most people would consider a massage, a long run, or curling up with a good book after a stressful workweek a perfect moment.

We all experience joy in unique ways, which explains why your perfect moments in each of these areas will look different than everyone else's moments.

Regardless of what your perfect moments look like, your goal should be to create and enjoy small moments before aiming for large—that is, expensive—moments. Like learning to crawl before you walk, starting small allows you to begin building your ideal life without breaking the bank. We call this "dreaming in stages."

DREAMING IN STAGES

Knowing that you can begin living a perfect life today, what should you do if the perfect moments you want aren't currently supported by your wealth? The approach we recommend is to start with small moments and plan for the larger ones.

In other words, you have to dream in stages.

We face this issue sometimes with clients who want the jet-setting lifestyle or the million-dollar beach house but can't afford those luxuries yet. Instead of shutting down their dreams, we focus on perfect moments they can have next week and create a plan to help them achieve their long-term goals once they've implemented the mechanics of money and created the wealth necessary to support those aims.

The moments they create in the short term are simple, inexpensive, and reinforce the idea that Life.Perfected. is worth pursuing. If you want to enjoy a perfect moment with your spouse and kids, you don't have to plan an expensive family vacation, when a picnic at the local park can be a perfect moment that is cheap and stress-free.

As you approach each day, adopt the simple appreciation of life that your eight-year-old self had. This mindset empowers you to create more perfect moments than if you simply dwell on more ambitious moments beyond your reach. When you shift your thinking in this way, you'll enjoy life's mundane moments a lot more, because they'll be offset by the joy of the perfect moments you're constantly creating.

RYAN PETERSON

My daughter Hailey is a talented actress. When we first discussed Life.Perfected., she told me that her ideal life involved winning an Oscar for best actress. We began to outline the journey she could take toward that lofty goal. The first step was envisioning a perfect moment she could have in the next month that would start her down the Oscar-winning path. She mentioned that when her high school play finished, she wanted to be in a play with me at our local community theater before she went to college. Not only would this moment allow us to spend time together, but it also lined up with her path to winning an Oscar. As the saying goes, "The best way to eat an elephant is one bite at a time."

When you dream in stages and create perfect moments along your journey, you can enjoy a life of perfection even if you never buy that private jet or win that Oscar.

So far, we've explored what an ideal life is:

A series of perfect moments that look different for everyone and sometimes have to be dreamed out in stages.

Now we'll explore how you discover what perfection means to you.

THE FOUR BIG QUESTIONS

As we've discussed, envisioning your ideal life can be overwhelming, which is why we broke that large, nebulous time span of life down into perfect moments that we can create. These moments can add up to create perfect days.

What does a perfect day look like to you?

Close your eyes and imagine living a perfect day. You can be anywhere, with anyone, doing anything you want. With this picture in your mind, answer the questions on the following pages and write down your answers.

Do this exercise yourself the first time to explore your own thoughts and goals, then share it with family and go through the exercise with them. You're going to learn things about yourself you never articulated before, and when you share it with your family, you'll learn things about them you never knew. We both did.

1. WHERE ARE YOU?

Be as specific as possible. Don't just say "the beach." Name the beach, envision the weather, the time of day, describe the scene, and so on.

....

2. WHO ARE YOU WITH?

The people you surround yourself with on a perfect day offer an important clue to your ideal life. Again, aim for specificity here. Don't say "friends" or "family." Name those people and see them in your mind.

....

3. WHAT ARE YOU DOING?

If you're at your favorite beach, are you reading a book by the pool, surfing, scuba diving, fishing, or playing with the kids in the ocean? More importantly, think about why you see yourself doing this activity in this place.

....

4. HOW DO YOU FEEL?

This answer shapes your ideal life more than anything. How do you feel at the end of a perfect day when your head hits the pillow? The feeling you have—relaxation, contentment, exhilaration, pride, and satisfaction—will be the feeling you seek in most perfect moments. Your location, activities, and companions might change, but if you're a thrill seeker, for example, you will seek out perfect moments that thrill you.

....

The answers to these questions are the building blocks of your Life.Perfected. But four blocks aren't enough. We need more, so we're giving you homework. After you've finished the first round of answers, revisit this exercise over the following few days and explore other perfect days in four categories:

1. With your family or friends
2. On your own
3. In your career
4. For charity or faith

There are blank lines at the end of this chapter for you to write down your answers.

Most people will answer the first time with their family in mind, but remember that we're trying to create perfect moments in every aspect of our lives, not just with family.

Finally, when you have four perfect days planned, go back and start the exercise over with the first category. Envision another perfect day with your family, for you personally, in your career, and for charity. This will require you to stretch your thinking and explore what Life.Perfected. looks like to you in a meaningful, multifaceted way. Your goal should be to create at least three perfect days in each category—twelve perfect days total.

We want you to go in depth with this exercise to discover your values, and then use your money in a way that allows you to live more of your life within those values.

Creating at least twelve perfect days also allows you to see the perfect moments you could create along your journey. If each of your perfect days involves relaxation, for example, you should seek to consistently create moments where you're perfectly relaxed. That could mean reading a book every evening or scheduling a monthly massage.

If you're struggling to envision a perfect day, use this trick to kick-start your imagination: picture yourself on your deathbed saying these words, "I wish I had spent more time..."

How would you finish that sentence? It probably isn't "at the office" or "trying to make money." Most likely it's "with my family" or "traveling the world" or "helping others."

Your answer will give you a starting point for exploring these four questions.

THE OBSTACLES TO LIFE.PERFECTED.

Now that you understand what an ideal life is and how to

discover yours, what's stopping you from living that life today? It should be easy to get started, right?

It turns out there are several obstacles that hold people back from a life of perfection. If you're not diligent about avoiding these traps, you'll find yourself bogged down by work or other responsibilities, wishing you could break free and live the life you want.

Let's touch on these obstacles quickly so you can identity and avoid each one.

DELAYED GRATIFICATION IS DANGEROUS

Basing your happiness on delayed gratification—that everything will be glorious at age fifty-five when you've got $5.5 million, for example—potentially leads to an unfulfilling life. Here's why:

- You must deal with the uncertainty that comes from hoping you'll get to enjoy your reward at "retirement age," while knowing that even tomorrow isn't guaranteed.
- When you're focused on saving for the future, you may skip perfect moments that could enrich your life in favor of a finish line that feels far away.
- Your goals will change during your life, so you must

seize perfect moments now while they're perfect for you. What's important to you at age thirty might not be important at forty or seventy.

Once you begin creating wealth and have a surplus of cash, you should absolutely indulge in small rewards, as long as you do so responsibly.

A client once said to us, "My wife wants to join a golf club, but she knows you're going to be mad at her for bringing it up because we can't afford it." Because he brought it up, we knew this client himself wanted to join the club along with his wife but wondered if he should delay that gratification until some future date when they could afford it.

Instead of shutting him down, we opened the door to this possibility.

"That sounds like a great idea," we told him. "If this is something that is meaningful to your family, let's figure out a reasonable way to make it happen."

The flip side is that instant gratification is also dangerous. You can't live like there's no tomorrow and blow all your money at once. There's a balance you have to walk between what you can afford to do now and what you must work to attain.

ARE YOU WASTING TIME AT WORK?

Almost all of us have to work for a living, and as we've seen, some of us fall into the trap of defining our lives by how much time we spend at the office. Investing our time there means we can't invest it in perfect moments with our families, for ourselves, or for charity.

Even if you're not married to your job, there are ways you can improve your efficiency at work and allow more time for perfect moments outside your career.

RYAN PETERSON

I learned two strategies for framing my time from The Strategic Coach founder, Dan Sullivan:

1. Find your Unique Ability and delegate everything else to others. When you focus on your Unique Ability, you're more productive and add more value to the world.

2. Implement an Entrepreneurial Time System. Focus on your results and the value you provide, not the time and effort you put in. Don't feel guilty if you get something done in five minutes that takes others ten hours. You can invest that time back into your work or use it to create perfect moments outside the office. (Note: Strategic Coach©, Unique Ability®, and Entrepreneurial Time System® are all property of The Strategic Coach Inc. and Dan Sullivan.)

Working smarter means getting the monkeys off your back—replying to emails, filling out reports, scheduling appointments, and so forth—so they don't slow you down. If you'd like to realize the power of delegation, we would encourage you to visit getleverage.com, a unique outsourcing company run by our friend Nick Sonnenberg (also check out his book, *Idea to Execution*).

Living an ideal life does require money, but money doesn't require you to be busy all the time. We want you to shake free of this money myth and focus on your results, so that poor time management at work doesn't become a stumbling block.

DON'T LET GUILT DRIVE YOUR DECISIONS

We've found that miserable people are often driven by guilt. They feel guilty that their boss isn't happy with their work, that they can't afford a nice vacation with their spouse, or that they aren't spending enough time with their kids. Their lives feel out of balance.

Guilt is closely tied to poor time management. People who feel guilty focus on the things they should be doing but can't, because they're bogged down elsewhere.

When these people start managing their time better and find the proper balance between work, family life, personal time, and charity, the feeling of guilt should begin to dissipate. They're able to enjoy what they're doing instead of stressing about what they're not doing.

Guilt also ties into the balance between delayed and instant gratification. Guilt can be found on either side of major purchases, whether it's buyer's remorse after a regretted purchase or the shame of not being able to provide a certain luxury for your family. The good news is that proper planning for large purchases can remove guilt from the equation.

No matter where it originates, guilt should not drive your decision making.

Guilt-driven people can miss opportunities for perfect moments because they think they don't deserve happiness. They may also overcompensate for guilt with reckless spending.

If your guilt is holding you back, take steps to address it. You won't be able to live the life of your dreams until you overcome guilt's detrimental economic and emotional impact.

LIFE.PERFECTED. ISN'T ABOUT MONEY

In this chapter, you've seen why an ideal life is not defined by your wealth. Money is simply a tool that enables you to enjoy perfect moments that may require more cash than the ones you enjoyed previously. Focusing on the tool at the expense of what you're building can lead to a hollow life, as Scooter Braun's story illustrates below.

If you don't know Braun, he's the man who discovered artists such as Justin Bieber. He shared on Lewis Howes's podcast, *The School of Greatness*, that when he was young and hustling, he decided he wanted to make a billion dollars. He just knew that if he was a billionaire, life would be perfect.

Somewhere along the way, Braun met someone who had everything he wanted but wasn't a billionaire, so he adjusted his number. This new, more achievable number reinvigorated Braun's determination to eventually make the new number his reality.

One day, as Braun was driving down the freeway, his business manager called to tell him he'd finally reached his number. In what should have been a moment of euphoria, Braun remembered hanging up the phone and feeling completely empty. The only thought going through his mind was, "What do I do now that I've achieved this goal?"

He called his dad for advice. After the shock of hearing his son's net worth wore off, he asked Braun, "What are you doing when you're at your absolute happiest?"

Braun shared that he was happiest when he was interacting with fans of his artists, whether through ticket giveaways or by replying to them on social media.

"Do more of that," his dad told him. "Understand that

the wealth is part of your job. The happiness is the time you take because your job has given you that freedom."

"I work my ass off," Braun told Howes, "for the moments that mean something."

When you make life about a number, you're going to feel empty when you reach it. But when you make life about the journey to reach that number and the perfect moments you have along the way, you'll already be fulfilled by the time you reach it. Hitting that number will simply enhance the beautiful life you've already built for yourself.

Now that you understand the "why" behind creating wealth, you're ready to begin building it. Our next step is to give you the truth about how money works.

LAY YOUR FINANCIAL FOUNDATION

Someone's sitting in the shade today because
someone planted a tree a long time ago.

WARREN BUFFETT

Zig Ziglar is famous for saying, "If it's going to be, it's up to me."

When it comes to understanding the mechanics of money, Ziglar's words ring especially true. Learning how money works is a responsibility that falls on your shoulders. Unless your parents were financial advisors, you probably didn't grow up reading *Rich Dad, Poor Dad* or studying the stock market. You might've taken an economics class, but overworked school teachers aren't equipped to provide students with a financial education.

There's also an emotional side to money that rarely gets discussed, but when you study the history of lottery winners and learn that one-third of them eventually declare bankruptcy, you can see that wealth isn't built merely of dollars and cents. Being unable to cope with wins and losses or spending impulsively will crack even the largest nest eggs.

Creating and managing wealth seems like a vast and complicated topic to most people, which explains why so many of us treat it like religion and politics at the dinner table.

But burying your head in the sand is not an option if you want to live your ideal life. You must take the initiative and teach yourself in order to lay a financial foundation. In this chapter, we're going to cover some fundamental financial concepts and begin to reshape how you think about money. Only after the foundation is laid can we progress to the mechanics of money.

Thankfully, learning how money works is not as difficult as you might believe. It's like learning to speak another language—everything may feel foreign at first, but if you start small and stack new concepts on that foundation, eventually you'll be fluent.

IN ORDER TO CARE, YOU HAVE TO LEARN

One question we get a lot is, "Do I really need a financial advisor?"

When potential clients ask us this, we reply that managing their finances requires the three Ts: time, talent, and temperament. Anyone can develop the talent if they have the time, so it comes down to whether they have the right temperament for managing money.

You have to consider whether you'd be happy tracking tax changes and monitoring stock market movement, or if you'd rather outsource that work to an advisor. Either way, you must become confident in your own financial literacy for one important reason: nobody will ever care about your money as much as you.

Let us be clear, if we were your advisors, we would care deeply for you and work to help you grow and manage your wealth, but at the end of the day, it's impossible for us to care as much as you do. It's *your* money that you've sweated, saved, and sacrificed for over the years.

You're naturally going to care more than anyone else what happens to that money, but in order to be a good caretaker, you must first understand how money works. Once you have that level of understanding, you can then put your money to work for you.

It's similar to becoming a parent—to adequately care for your child, you're going to learn everything you can about childcare. Even if you hire a nanny or a babysitter, you still need that knowledge to ensure your child is receiving the best care possible.

Knowing you need to lay a financial foundation is an important first step. The trap that many people fall into is seeking out and following advice from the wrong sources.

DON'T BELIEVE THE HYPE

Lacking a formal financial education, many people turn to the Internet, magazines, books, radio, and TV for their financial advice. What they don't realize is that mainstream media is designed to sell advertising. Popular products and programs aren't concerned with your money but rather the money they're making through ad revenue.

As we all know, successful advertising grabs the attention of as many people as possible. Popular media grabs your attention by chasing the latest trends, having bombastic on-air personalities, and promising fail-proof, get-rich-quick schemes.

Any tactic that gets you to click, buy, subscribe, or tune in can and will be used. When considering the advice of well-known financial gurus, ask yourself two questions:

1. Whom does this person work for?
2. What is their motivation?

Most famous financial personalities want to build a consumer base that will buy books, programs, and seminar tickets. That's not to say everything these "gurus" say is bad advice—we wouldn't include them by name in this book if they were—just that you must always consider the source.

Even the most trusted, well-known financial authors should have their advice inspected for bias because, after all, their goal is to sell books. The advice they offer also has to be generalized to appeal to a mass audience, so while the methods they describe may work for the majority of people, it won't work for everyone.

OPT FOR A MERIT-BASED APPROACH

Here's another question we use with our clients to help them separate fact from hype: Is this advice based on marketing or merit?

Most of the advice you get from the media and large financial firms is based on marketing because there's a product on the shelf they're hoping you'll buy.

An easy way to tell the difference is that if you get a sales pitch for whatever approach they're advocating, it's marketing. A merit-based approach—one based on sound financial hypothesis tested by financial experts—doesn't need to be sold. You've heard your advisors say it before, and it's true, "Past performance is not an indicator of future results."

We know that the old-fashioned, back-to-basics approach may sound boring. While it's true our approach isn't flashy, we have another word to describe our strategy and methodology to building wealth long term: smart.

It seems like a no-brainer to say that the most prudent path is the one with the highest probability of success, but as advisors, we're constantly pushing back against the bad advice that our clients believe because they've bought into the hype.

We had a client who'd been with us for many years and we were working to turn his wealth into a stream of retirement income. The strategy we shared with him probably sounded "boring" because he had a more "exciting" strategy in mind. He wanted to find twelve stocks that paid a dividend of at least 8 percent and live off the dividend. We told him that sounded like a great idea so long as he could bring us evidence from a reputable source that showed this strategy had a high probability of success over the next thirty years while he was in retirement.

The problem was that no CFP®, university research department, or member of the academic community that we've ever heard of would say it's prudent to live off the dividends of twelve stocks. As we'll see in chapter 3, when you run the numbers, you find that this strategy has a very low chance of success.

The client simply liked his strategy more than ours. We couldn't support his idea without merit to back it up, and ultimately he decided to take his money elsewhere.

His story illustrates the importance of validating advice once you've considered the conflicts of interest and motivation of the person sharing it. Unbiased advice can still be harmful if it's not independently verified and backed up by financial science.

UNDERSTANDING YOUR MONEY

An important step in laying your financial foundation is knowing where your money comes from and where it's going. Envision your personal finances as a business and you're the owner. Business owners need to know where every dollar is being spent within their company so they can make informed decisions.

What's funny is that most of our clients are business owners, and yet we frequently find a disconnect between how they manage their business and how they manage their personal finances. If you do it correctly, the process is the same in both areas of your life.

There are two main reporting instruments that every business should be using to make decisions: a balance sheet and an income statement.

A personal balance sheet (also called a net worth statement) is simply what you own minus what you owe. What's left over is your net worth.

A personal income statement, or profit and loss statement, reflects how much money is coming in from various sources—interest, earnings, wages, and so forth—and how much is going out for expenses. Public companies publish their profits and losses in annual reports that are hundreds of pages long, but the key figures can be condensed to a couple of pages.

With clients, we start with these two instruments because any short- or long-term goals we set will be based on the facts we see reflected in those numbers.

Most people rely on the income statement when they're young because they don't yet have assets to put on a balance sheet. They make decisions based on the money they're making and the money they're spending to live the life they want. If they're lucky, they might have leftover money each month to put in savings.

For those who employ the rules of money throughout their life, the balance sheet will become more important over time as their assets grow and begin to generate side income streams that add money back into the pot. The eventual goal is to shift all decision making to the balance sheet once it becomes the sole driver of their income. For a sample balance sheet and income statement, visit LifePerfected.com/book.

Income generated completely off your balance sheet that covers all your lifestyle expense needs is true financial independence.

THINK LONG TERM

Running your personal finances like a business starts with looking beyond your current situation. Successful business owners don't just focus on short-term concerns such as how much income is being generated or how much credit they have available. They're also looking at the big picture and making decisions that impact their long-term goals, which could range from opening multiple locations to getting bought out by a larger company.

Your long-term goal is to live the life of your dreams, and to do that, your decision making eventually has to shift to your balance sheet. That shift is preceded by a shift in how you think about money and is followed up with patience and diligence.

With your income statement and balance sheet in hand, you can put yourself in the mind of a business owner if you look at the data and ask yourself these questions:

- How does my income look compared to last month?
- If I brought in less money, how can I cut expenses?
- If I brought in more money, can I use that excess to create assets?
- What's a goal I can set for next month (less spending, more investing, etc.)?

- Within the next twelve months, what assets can I create or grow?

The answers to these questions can be small, and the process by which you answer them can be fun. In fact, you can even make a game out of it if you want.

RYAN HEATH

My middle child, Reed, is a shoe fanatic and has started making money selling shoes to his friends. While we were shopping at the Nike outlet store in Orlando, I told him I'd buy two pairs of shoes that he could sell and we'd split the profits. He found two pairs for $80 total that were selling for $475 total on the Finish Line website. He told me he could sell them each for $150, leaving us to split $220 in profit, so I bought the shoes for him.

Through this exercise, I'm teaching him to think long term about investing and how his money can work for him. On the flip side, I'm also teaching him to recognize poor uses of his money, such as buying that $15 pair of Mickey Mouse ears that he'd never wear after we left the park. Once he thought about it, he said, "You're right. I didn't need those. It was a stupid buy." He makes plenty of other stupid buys, but that was a nice moment of reflection.

Running your personal finances like a business shouldn't be painful. If you adopt the right mindset and find fun ways to add assets to your balance sheet, it should be enjoyable.

MINIMIZE THE TAX DRAIN

Taxes factor so much into the mechanics of money that we'll cover them in depth in chapter 5, but we'll touch on them here to kick-start your thinking.

We like to tell clients that we're all business partners with the United States government, and as such, we're legally required to share profits we make with the federal government. Taxes can be a major drain on your wealth, but there are some steps you can take to lessen the burden.

You lessen that burden by practicing tax avoidance. To explain that concept, here's a story we like to share from an essay titled "Thoughts on Legitimate Tax Avoidance" that was written by former Supreme Court Justice Louis Brandeis:

"I live in Alexandria, Virginia. Near the Supreme Court chambers is a toll bridge across the Potomac. When in a rush, I pay the dollar toll and get home early. However, I usually drive outside the downtown section of the city and cross the Potomac on a free bridge.

"If I went over the toll bridge and through the barrier without paying the toll, I would be committing tax evasion. If, however, I drive the extra mile outside the city of Washington and take the free bridge, I am using a legitimate, logical, and suitable method of tax avoidance, and I am performing a useful social service by doing so.

"For my tax evasion, I should be punished.

"For my tax avoidance, I should be commended."

If you want to take the toll bridge home—essentially doing zero tax planning and just paying what you owe quickly to have it over with—that's your prerogative.

But if you're trying to put your money to work, and you're clipping 30 to 50 cents off the top of every dollar in taxes, the productivity and output of that money is seriously weakened.

With simple strategies such as deducting your mortgage interest, or taking a 401(k) deduction, you can reduce your tax bill and keep more of your dollar's earning value for you.

Like we said earlier, minimizing your tax drain starts with you. Nobody from the IRS is going to come to your house and teach you how to reduce your taxes. Even if you have a phenomenal CPA, you shouldn't rely on them to save you money.

CPAs are some of the most overworked and underappreciated people in the financial services industry. Their job is immensely complex and filled with mountains of paperwork, unforgiving deadlines, and endless filings. There is no doubt that most of them could devise tax strategies to help you to pay less if they just had more hours in the day.

We once introduced an idea to a client and his tax advisor that could result in millions of dollars in tax benefit over a five-year period. The client was furious that after twenty years of working together, his advisor hadn't suggested the strategy to him previously. We had to remind him that the priorities of a CPA are to make sure filings are done correctly and that all deadlines are met. Advisors don't always have the bandwidth to identify new strategies.

Don't assume that you're taking advantage of all the tax reduction or avoidance strategies available to you just because you have a CPA or tax attorney. You either need to educate yourself or find the right mix of advisors who can strategize and implement the best tax tactics for you.

PROTECT YOUR WEALTH FROM PREDATORS

Taxes are a type of predator looking to eat away at your wealth, but because we're legally bound to pay them, we can't evade them entirely. There are, however, other predators who will come knocking at your door once your wealth accumulates.

If you're a business owner, you need the right legal structures to protect yourself from lawsuits, judgments, and creditors. If your assets are exposed, legally speaking, they're vulnerable to being picked off whenever someone files a lawsuit or you fall behind on your payments and the creditors come calling.

Predators don't always sneak in the back door. Sometimes we invite them in through the front door not knowing they're wolves in sheep's clothing. This could be an advisor or financial "guru" claiming he has the next great investment strategy. Going back to our discussion of biased information sources, these are the mainstream media personalities hyping up the next hot stock or the gold bugs who come out of the woodwork during uncertain times when people are looking for reassurance that their wealth is safe.

If you think the wealthy are putting the majority of their money into private equity deals and other flashy investments, think again. Their core is often boring and predictable. Often, the "unwealthy" are the ones looking for thrills and sinking large amounts of money and risk into investments that have a very low chance of getting a return. Don't put large amounts of money into deals with a high amount of risk because you may end up with nothing.

Will Rogers said it best: "I am not so much concerned with the return *on* capital as I am with the return *of* capital."

You have to keep the predators away from your wealth and stay in the middle of the predictable road to prosperity to remain wealthy.

As harsh as it sounds, friends and family members can also be predators. There are countless stories of famous athletes who invested in a friend's business only for the business to go under and that investment to evaporate. When it's a friend or family member asking, our judgment becomes clouded by emotion, and we invest too much money or get involved with a venture that's outside our interests.

Those who are wealthy and wise don't shut themselves off to investing in the ventures of loved ones; they just do it at an amount they can afford to lose.

Nobody wants to deal with the stress of worrying about their wealth or the pain of actually having it swiped by predators. Those hassles aren't included in an ideal life.

Take the steps on the front end to secure your wealth from predators, whether that means educating yourself or assembling a team of advisors and attorneys to help you. Whatever work you put in will be worth it to avoid dealing with the fallout on the back end.

DON'T SPOIL YOUR KIDS

As wealth begins to accumulate, it can pose a difficult dilemma. When you can give your child expensive gifts or experiences, should you? How much is too much?

Warren Buffett had the right idea when he answered that question this way: "Give your kids enough to do anything they want but not so much they can do nothing."

We both grew up in middle-class families where food was on the table every night, but when our parents said we couldn't do something—such as go to Disney World—they meant we literally didn't have enough money to cover that trip and pay the bills.

As Robert Frank discusses in his book *Richistan*, the

wealthy must learn to say, "We aren't going to do that," rather than "We can't do that."

When you love your kids, it's easy to spoil them. The challenge is finding the balance between letting them enjoy money and letting it consume them. Going overboard with your kids can make them lazy, cause them to lose touch with reality, and shift their perspective on what's important in life. It's a slippery slope you should avoid at all costs.

RYAN HEATH

When my oldest child, River, was about to turn sixteen, we started talking about a car. I never had a car growing up, so part of me wanted to go all out and get him something over the top. But I also knew that wasn't the most prudent decision. Amazingly, it was my son who set me straight. "You know, Dad," he said, "being that this is my first car, something older, in decent shape would probably be a good idea." I think he was worried about the pressure of driving something too nice. It's funny that it took the reasonableness of a teenager to snap me back to reality.

Include your children in the goal-setting exercise we discussed earlier. If they help your family meet its goal next month, take everyone out for a nice dinner, or sock away money for a few months and go on a nice trip. If you make it a game and make it fun, children will be more eager to participate and learn. Even if you decide to invest that extra income, let your children help decide on the investment.

Our company's founder, Dr. Philips, has always been charitable. Early on, he decided to incorporate his children, who are now grown, into the process of selecting causes to support and where money should be given. Their efforts have grown so large that his daughter now works full time seeking out new organizations to support.

Dr. Philips's efforts helped keep his children grounded even as they grew up surrounded by wealth. He took the important step of talking to his kids about money rather than avoiding it like so many families do. The balance sheet is not so sacred that it should be kept from your children. If you're more worried about exposing your lack of financial knowledge when you talk to your kids about money, consider that another reason to learn the mechanics of money and develop a proper framework for that conversation.

However you invest in your kids, remember these important words from Warren Buffett: "The greatest gift you can give your kids is love."

RYAN PETERSON

When I was being trained as a mentor for the Big Brothers Big Sisters organization, they told me the most successful mentors opt for fun experiences such as bike rides or flying a kite with their little brother or sister, not expensive meals or trips to the movies. The same is true when you have kids of your own—perfect moments don't have to come from your bank account. They can happen in a park, on the way home from school, or in the backyard on a fall night when you're raking up leaves. It's about spending time together, not spending money.

RESET THE SCRIPT

As we've been laying the foundation for understanding the mechanics of money in this chapter, our goal has been to reset how you think about wealth. We want to wipe away any preconceived notions you have and align your thinking around this truth:

Creating wealth is simple, but it's not easy.

We talk to many people who think the only way to get rich is to have something happen in their life—win the lottery, invent the next billion-dollar app, or inherit their family's fortune. They believe there's a tremendous amount of luck involved and that most wealthy people were just in the right place at the right time.

A small percentage of people get wealthy this way, but because their stories are sensational, we hear about them and that pathway becomes the dominant one in our minds.

Most people become wealthy by working hard for a long time. We know, that's a vanilla answer among all the crazy flavors that are available. The truth is, there's no guaranteed path to long-term wealth. You can opt for the easiest path and hope the small chance of success works in your favor, or you can choose the more difficult path that comes with the highest probability of success. We hope the choice seems obvious.

We also want to change how you think once you start accumulating wealth. Designing your ideal life is meant to instill purpose into the creation of your wealth. Without it, you'll be just mindlessly chasing a number.

RYAN HEATH

The executives I saw who measured their wealth against that of others were seldom happy. They'd say things like, "I'm the fifth-highest paid person in this company." I would wonder what happened when they became the highest-paid person in the company. Would they turn their sights to their entire industry, the country, or even the world? It seemed fruitless to seek validation in this manner because there'd always be someone ahead of them.

People who spend their life chasing the carrot of money, status, or power too often fail to convert that capital into new experiences and opportunities. You don't hear people on their deathbed wishing they'd spent more time at the office or closed another deal. You do hear people wishing they'd spent more time with family or enjoyed the experiences their wealth afforded them. They regret creating wealth without a purpose.

As we dive deeper into the mechanics of money in the coming chapters, keep your purpose front and center. If you do, we believe you'll finish this book with a refreshed mindset and the proper perspective for using wealth once you have it.

PINKY RINGS & MINIVANS

One struggle many people face when they're trying to create wealth is deciding whether to save for tomorrow or spend today.

Early in our lives, many of us have limited discretionary income left over each month. Our disciplined, long-term side knows we should put that money aside so we can move closer to our ideal life. Our fun-loving, short-term side sees other ways to spend our money that can provide instant gratification.

You might expect us to say the first option is the right choice, but honestly, there is no right or wrong answer, and we believe an appropriately balanced approach is the best answer. We never judge our clients for their spending choices. We do, however, point out how those decisions impact their ability to meet long-term goals.

RYAN PETERSON

A young family paid me to create a financial plan for the few hundred dollars of discretionary income they had each month, so I designed a plan that met their goals and scheduled a second meeting to discuss it with them. When I sat down, I asked them if anything about their financial situation had changed since our last meeting.

The husband said, "My wife bought me some jewelry for my birthday," and he flashed me this pinky ring with a diamond and black onyx.

The pinky ring wiped out the $1,200 they had in cash reserves. Undeterred, I asked them if anything else had changed. That's when they informed me of the minivan purchase that completely wiped out their monthly discretionary income.

In between our meetings, two purchases obliterated their chance of putting money toward their goals. But the husband got to drive his family around in their new minivan with his pinky ring up on the steering wheel, which made him and his family happy (at least temporarily). I realized that despite my frustration, it wasn't my place to judge their spending decisions. My role as a financial advisor is to help people establish life goals that are important to them and make them aware of the consequences—both positive and negative—of their financial behavior.

The upside is that this experience gave me the title for our next book, *Pinky Rings & Minivans.*

We all have a choice to make. Some days, saving your discretionary income or using it to create assets will feel like the wrong choice. Remind yourself of these truths:

1. Building wealth is simple, but it's not easy.
2. Building wealth requires hard work over a long period of time.

We can't tell you how long it will take to achieve financial independence or how difficult the road will be for you. But if you make it a priority to live those moments of perfection when you can, you'll see that the sacrifice to achieve Life.Perfected. is worth it.

CONTINUE TO LEARN AND GROW

Whether you plan to work with advisors or employ the mechanics of money on your own, building wealth requires a basic understanding of both finances in general and your own situation. Throughout this chapter, we've laid a financial foundation that gives you the basis needed to understand the rules of money in these four areas:

1. Income planning
2. Investing
3. Tax planning
4. Wealth transference

We can show you how to employ the rules of money to build your wealth and enable your ideal life, but it's your job to maintain what you're going to build.

We see two main ways you can do that: assemble a top-notch team and read and apply what you learn.

The right team can help you create a plan designed to achieve your goals. If you have the three Ts necessary to manage your own wealth—time, talent, and temperament—we'd encourage you not to skip this section in case you ever do need to call on outside help.

We've talked already about how the right blend of experts and advisors can help you take full advantage of the mechanics of money. Seek out CPAs, financial advisors, and attorneys who are reputable and have proven track records. Interview them to determine:

- How comfortable you feel with each one
- How competent they are in their respective field
- How confident you feel trusting them with your goals

Successful entrepreneurs demonstrate the importance of having different advisors to help them manage the various aspects of their business. Famous athletes employ coaches to manage different areas of their game (e.g., a golf swing or jump shot), and advisors from outside their circle of influence who can provide them with sound, objective advice.

Our advice would be that if you're looking to hire advisors, concern yourself with the quality of their work and not the cost. In financial services, like many industries, you get what you pay for most times. If you find someone with a unique ability to help grow your wealth or minimize your tax costs, don't be afraid to invest in yourself and your future.

You must also realize that you're paying an advisor to be honest, not necessarily nice. While it's important to have a good working relationship with your advisor, it's also critical that you work with someone who's not afraid to give you "tough love" when you're cheating yourself.

Finally, never underestimate the power of gut instinct when selecting advisors. If something about the advisor doesn't feel right when you interview them, move on until you find one you can completely trust.

You should also invest in yourself by continuing to read and study the mechanics of money. We have four decades of experience in this industry between us, and we both spend hours each week reading books, articles, and studies. We talk to people we know who are living their ideal life and ask them for advice. Our job demands that we consistently absorb new information in order to best serve our clients. But even if we weren't in this industry, we'd continue to learn because a Life.Perfected. requires growth.

One book we specifically recommend is *The Richest Man in Babylon* by George Samuel Clason. Despite being published in 1926, this book shares timeless parables about the different concepts of money and the discipline of creating wealth. We've given it out to hundreds of people over the years because it speaks to the mindset you need to create wealth, which is just as important as the mechanics of money.

Stay away from the generic, watered-down advice that floods TV, radio, and best seller bookshelves. As discussed previously, some of it is good, but if you do utilize those information sources, be sure to test the advice you get against the principles in this book or against the advice of your team.

Once you've committed to continual education and growth, you're ready to begin studying the mechanics of money at its starting point: income planning.

INCOME PLANNING

*If you don't find a way to make money while
you sleep, you will work until you die.*

WARREN BUFFETT

If there's one word we hesitate to use in this book, it's
retirement. This word represents an outdated idea that
doesn't apply in today's world like it once did.

We can't imagine a day in the future where we'll completely retire from all types of work, and we're sure many
of you feel the same way. Even if it's just volunteering or
charitable work, we'll most likely be doing something to
keep active until the day we die.

Instead of thinking about the day you retire, we encourage

you to think of the day when you achieve financial independence. When you have a reliable stream of income regardless of the hours you work, we call that Financial Independence Day.

On that day, you will work because you want to, not because you have to. Now your balance sheet is working for you, allowing you to enjoy your Life.Perfected.

As joyous as Financial Independence Day is for those who work hard and get to celebrate it, the road to that day can be lined with questions and insecurity:

- How much do I need?
- What's the best way to create solid income?
- How will I know when I'm financially independent?

Financial Independence Day is not impossible to achieve, but it can feel far away for those who misunderstand the process. Creating financial independence is possible if you're willing to learn, make sacrifices, and build good habits. Remember, building wealth you can live off is simple, but it's not easy.

Here are some habits that can make it easier to create income during your working years.

INCREMENTAL CHANGES LEAD TO BIG RESULTS

In his book *The Tipping Point*, Malcolm Gladwell talks about small changes that have a massive impact over time. We both came away from that book with the same thought: Those who spend all their money will never be wealthy, but those who spend most of their money can be wealthy if they're smart with what's left over.

Many people we talk with, especially those who are younger, believe that accumulating wealth only comes from making big changes to their situation. All they see is sacrificing fun in the name of saving money for a day that seems so far away.

They're right. Saving for financial independence does require sacrifice. But as we know, you can still save and enjoy moments of perfection along the way.

Where they're wrong is that wealth isn't usually built off massive, five- or six-figure investments. It happens as a result of small choices stretched out over decades. Saving $200 instead of $50 from every paycheck doesn't seem like much now, but fast forward many years into the future and your savings will reach a tipping point where its growth can skyrocket.

In his two most recent books, *Money: Master the Game* and

Unshakeable, Tony Robbins hammers home the power of compound interest. When we first read that, we thought, "Everyone already knows about compound interest." Einstein called it the eighth wonder of the world. Why even bring it up?

But when we talk with clients and other people we know and realize that although those in the financial services industry understand compound interest, few others do.

If you're just starting out, compound interest could be the small change you make now that creates a tipping point with your wealth in the future. Just remember that when you choose a prudent path to financial independence, you aren't going to strike it rich after a couple of years. You need discipline and patience to one day reach the finish line.

No matter where you are on the path to financial independence, here are some other simple but powerful strategies that can help you one day reach your goal.

KEEP INCOME AND EXPENSES IN BALANCE

A client of ours who is a young and successful physician asked us recently if he should save the $8,000 of monthly income he was earning from his new practice location.

As his advisors, we reassured him that saving was a brilliant idea.

We were thrilled with his choice because it's not usually what we see in situations where a person's income suddenly increases. Too often, needs that were once only dreamed of—such as a luxury automobile—become the new standard of living for people who see big influxes of money. As their income increases, their lifestyle causes their needs (i.e., expenses) to increase to levels that can outstrip their original income levels, as this illustration demonstrates.

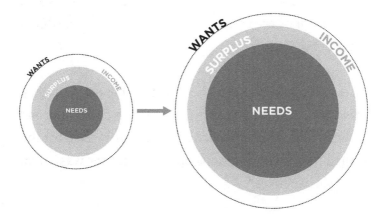

When income and expenses increase at the same rate, wealth is difficult to achieve. Expenses can increase, of course, as long as they grow slower than income. When this happens, you're left with an ever-widening surplus of money to invest in your future, and you can still enjoy the fruits of your extra income with reasonable expense increases.

Two other clients, a husband and wife, shared with us that the husband received a $100,000 bonus after his public company had a successful quarter. A while later, we saw the wife driving a new Mercedes-Benz and sporting a $25,000 diamond ring.

If we had to guess, these two lavish purchases might have caused some jealousy among their friends, or at least didn't make a favorable impression. If they're like us, their friends offered the obligatory compliment and didn't think about it again.

Instead of adding value to their relationships or improving their social standing, it's likely those purchases only had a negative impact on the couple's ability to save for the future. It was a tremendous opportunity they wasted on "lifestyle expenses."

Sadly, their story is not unique. Whether it's a minivan and a pinky ring, or a Mercedes-Benz and a diamond ring, the impulse to indulge snares all of us at times.

Before you get upset, we're not saying that an ideal life

can't include splurge purchases. We like nice things too, and we're merely emphasizing the importance of balance. If the couple had saved $85,000 from that bonus and spent $15,000 on a ring or a car, we would've cheered that balance. But spending 100 percent is a decision that's totally unbalanced.

RYAN PETERSON

I like nice cars and so do my boys. Napa Valley draws a lot of tourism from the wealthy crowd, and it's not unusual to see a Ferrari or Lamborghini while we're out driving around. The boys' reaction is usually, "Wow, they must be rich."

There are exceptionally wealthy people who can afford whatever they desire, but over the years, I've met just as many people whose life would crumble if they missed one paycheck. It can sometimes be difficult to tell the difference between someone who's truly wealthy and a pretender who's living above their means.

Unfortunately, people tend to see the material possessions and make quick judgments, which makes it more difficult to explain the importance of keeping your income and expenses in balance. But that's still a conversation worth having.

An advisor I met early in my career explained it this way: "An inflated ego makes you buy things that you don't need, with money that you don't have, to try to impress people who don't even like you."

Many people believe they're wealthy because they make a lot of money, but cash flow doesn't always equal wealth. If your wages stopped today and you could continue with your current lifestyle, you're wealthy. If you couldn't, you're not wealthy...yet.

AUTOMATE YOUR SAVING

We hate budgets—they're boring, stressful, and nobody wants to stick to them. When it comes to saving for Financial Independence Day, you want to automate your habits, not budget your money. If you see the income that you should be saving, you'll be tempted to spend it, and we all know that spending can be a lot more fun than saving.

But if you take steps to automate your savings process, then you'll never see the money that is earmarked for savings and won't be tempted to spend it.

Vanguard published research in 2014 showing that when employers automatically enrolled employees in 401(k) plans rather than making opt-in voluntary, the participation rate rose from 42 percent to 91 percent. Not only that, but eight out of ten participants in the study increased their contribution over time, proving that saving becomes easier—even habitual—if it's out of sight, out of mind. With today's technology, we have the power to do that.

PERCEPTION ISN'T ALWAYS REALITY

In the same way that human beings tend to spend money rather than save it, we are all guilty of sharing overly positive versions of our reality:

- Golfers recall their great shots and not their shanks.
- Investors brag about the stock that produced a great return and keep quiet on the investments that lost money.
- Nobody ever comes back from Las Vegas a loser.

The danger comes in believing these rosy realities are the whole story, which leads us to feel like we're missing out on something. The fear of missing out (FOMO) causes us to jump from one investment to another, or stop paying the premiums on our life insurance before the insurance company pays us a dime. The stories others tell us are thrilling, and when FOMO kicks in, we foolishly go off chasing thrills of our own.

The strategies in this book for building wealth are effective, but as we've said, they're also boring. Don't always believe the hype you hear from others and give in to the temptation to chase thrills on the road to Financial Independence Day.

Listen to those you trust, stick to your strategy, and block out all the noise.

THE CHANGING FACE OF INCOME

These habits form a solid foundation on which to create the income you need to celebrate Financial Independence Day. So how do you create reliable income streams that can serve as the catalyst for your ideal life? One path we recommend is to purchase the income, and we'll cover what that means later in this chapter.

Another path that you're seeing more millennials opt for is building side businesses that provide income streams even while they sleep. The Internet has made it cheaper to manufacture and ship goods, accept online payments, and communicate with customers. In other words, it's never been easier to transform a "side hustle" into a profitable business that can match—or even exceed—your full-time income.

However, don't confuse "easier" with "easy." Creating profitable side income streams requires hard work. You might have to sacrifice sleep, hobbies, or time spent with family to work on developing, marketing, and selling your product or service.

One couple we know recently decided to buy into a pizza restaurant franchise. Soon after it opened, they decided to go on a date for dinner to check on their investment. When they arrived, it was so slammed that they ended up busing tables and helping in the kitchen. They were thrilled with the immediate success of the new venture, but they also realized they were going to have to roll up their sleeves and stay involved.

There are ways to make this process easier, though. In *The 4-Hour Workweek*, Tim Ferriss suggests tying your income needs to a specific project or goal.

For example, if your version of Life.Perfected. includes traveling more with your family, you could set a goal to travel two more times per year than you are now. Ferriss says you should then price that goal and seek to create that level of income with your side business. So rather than setting a lofty goal of earning $1 million in side income—which would be difficult to achieve and likely leave you discouraged—you can set a realistic goal of creating enough extra income to cover your travel costs.

It's possible to repeat this process enough that the income you create covers your expenses and allows you to purchase income for your financial independence.

Creating "twenty-first-century income" that steadily moves you toward a fully realized Life.Perfected. is necessary because the traditional path to financial independence—the one taken by millions of baby boomers decades ago—is increasingly harder to come by.

PENSIONS AND SOCIAL SECURITY ARE UNRELIABLE

When we started in finance more than twenty-five years ago, you had three main sources of retirement income:

1. Pensions
2. Social security
3. Personal savings

For most people, the most important legs were their pension and social security. As we know from history class, social security was enacted by the federal government in 1935 as part of Franklin D. Roosevelt's New Deal, so that people could retire at age sixty-five. Of course, the average life expectancy was 61 in 1935, so this program was really designed for people who lived way beyond average mortality.

The first pension was created in 1875 by the American Express Company, and by the time social security was introduced, 15 percent of America's workforce had a pension. The plan for millions of baby boomers was simple: once they turned sixty-five, they'd retire and live mainly off the set paycheck of their pension and social security income. Whatever shortfall existed with their income would be covered by personal savings.

Recent developments have severely stressed social security for anyone under fifty-five. With baby boomers taking social security in record numbers, there aren't enough people paying into the program to make it a reliable long-term option. Younger workers don't work at one company for forty years and collect a pension, and even if they did stay long term, they'd have a hard time finding an employer that still offers this benefit.

Forbes ran an article in 2012 (which we've linked at LifePerfected.com/book) about large companies such as General Motors shutting down or offloading their pension programs because they're expensive and difficult to manage. Many companies have chosen to offer only a 401(k) that lets them off the hook for providing a lifetime income stream to their retired employees.

These changes represent a dramatic shift in how people approach saving for financial independence. Not only is the path different, but the end date has shifted as well.

Sixty-five is no longer the magical age when we get to retire from work and begin enjoying life. With the burden of saving now on our shoulders, we're in control of our financial independence, and the sooner we achieve it, the better.

Until that day, we're going to enjoy moments of perfection that don't require significant wealth—time spent with family, traveling, or pursuing our passion, to name a few. Those moments will inform our ideal life, so that on the day we achieve independence, we don't have to worry about deciding what our financially free life looks like.

The shifting landscape offers another big takeaway—if the brilliant minds who run large corporate pension plans can't figure out income planning for employees, you shouldn't approach this process haphazardly. Income planning requires precision and care. A generic "save money and hope for the best" approach won't get the job done.

But why is this such a precarious position for these brilliant pension managers? It has a lot to do with a little-known concept called the lottery of returns.

THE LOTTERY OF RETURNS

Imagine you're planning a trip to Manhattan in January.

The night before leaving, while packing your bags, you wonder what the temperature will be. You search Google for "average annual temperature in Manhattan" and discover the average temperature throughout the year is 56°F, so you pack your bags accordingly. However, when you land the next day, you find the city battling a blizzard with subzero temperatures.

The flaw in your planning was relying solely on averages. What you should have done was pack for the current weather instead of the weather Manhattan usually gets.

This is the flaw of many people when building a financial independence plan: relying on average expected results. When we consider the current "economic weather" of low fixed rates and overvalued stocks, we have to plan more cautiously.

The truth is that investment returns don't come in equal installments, regardless of long-term averages, and this fact means EVERYTHING when you begin withdrawing money from your savings and investments.

Let's look at an example using the returns for the S&P 500 from 1989 to 2008.

FORWARD

YEAR	HYPOTHETICAL PORTFOLIO RETURN	WITHDRAWAL	END OF THE YEAR BALANCE
INITIAL BALANCE: $1,000,000			
1989	31.48%		$1,314,800
1990	-3.06%		$1,274,567
1991	30.23%		$1,659,868
1992	7.49%		$1,784,192
1993	9.97%		$1,962,076
1994	1.33%		$1,988,172
1995	37.20%		$2,727,772
1996	22.68%		$3,346,431
1997	33.10%		$4,454,100
1998	28.34%	No Withdrawal	$5,716,392
1999	20.89%		$6,910,547
2000	-9.03%		$6,286,524
2001	-11.85%		$5,541,571
2002	-21.97%		$4,324,088
2003	28.36%		$5,550,399
2004	10.74%		$6,146,512
2005	4.83%		$6,443,389
2006	15.61%		$7,449,202
2007	5.48%		$7,857,418
2008	-36.55%		$4,985,532
AVERAGE RETURN: 10.26%		TOTAL WITHDRAWAL:	$0

The average of these returns equals 10.26 percent, which is close to the long-term average of the S&P 500 Index. While it's fair to assume these long-term averages might happen again, it would be foolish to think these returns will happen in the same annual order every twenty years. This is what we call the lottery of returns.

To illustrate this concept, say you invested $1 million in an S&P 500 Index fund and got a 10.26 percent rate of return. How would things look different if you got to that average using the annual returns from 2008 to 1989, the reverse of what we just saw? Take a look.

BACKWARD

YEAR	HYPOTHETICAL PORTFOLIO RETURN	WITHDRAWAL	END OF THE YEAR BALANCE
INITIAL BALANCE: $1,000,000			
1989	-36.55%		$634,500
1990	5.48%		$669,270
1991	15.61%		$773,743
1992	4.83%		$811,115
1993	10.74%		$898,229
1994	28.36%		$1,152,967
1995	-21.97%		$899,660
1996	-11.85%		$793,050
1997	-9.03%		$721,438
1998	20.89%	No Withdrawal	$872,146
1999	28.34%		$1,119,312
2000	33.10%		$1,489,805
2001	22.68%		$1,827,693
2002	37.20%		$2,507,595
2003	1.33%		$2,540,946
2004	9.97%		$2,794,278
2005	7.49%		$3,003,569
2006	30.23%		$3,911,549
2007	-3.06%		$3,791,855
2008	31.48%		$4,985,532
AVERAGE RETURN: 10.26%		TOTAL WITHDRAWAL:	$0

FORWARD

YEAR	HYPOTHETICAL PORTFOLIO RETURN	WITHDRAWAL	END OF THE YEAR BALANCE
INITIAL BALANCE: $1,000,000			
1989	31.48%	$50,000	$1,249,060
1990	-3.06%	$51,500	$1,160,914
1991	30.23%	$53,045	$1,442,778
1992	7.49%	$54,636	$1,492,114
1993	9.97%	$56,275	$1,578,991
1994	1.33%	$57,963	$1,541,257
1995	37.20%	$59,702	$2,032,693
1996	22.68%	$61,493	$2,418,268
1997	33.10%	$63,338	$3,134,411
1998	28.34%	$65,238	$3,938,976
1999	20.89%	$67,195	$4,680,595
2000	-9.03%	$69,211	$4,194,975
2001	-11.85%	$71,288	$3,635,030
2002	-21.97%	$73,426	$2,779,119
2003	28.36%	$75,629	$3,470,200
2004	10.74%	$77,898	$3,756,634
2005	4.83%	$80,235	$3,853,969
2006	15.61%	$82,642	$4,360,031
2007	5.48%	$85,121	$4,509,174
2008	-36.55%	$87,675	$2,805,441
AVERAGE RETURN: 10.26%		TOTAL WITHDRAWAL:	$1,343,519

As you can see, the two scenarios take totally different paths but end at the same point. In fact, you could jumble these twenty annual returns into any combination and each one would end with the same result: a 10.26 percent average return and a final value of $4,985,532.

Here's where it gets interesting. What if we introduce an annual withdrawal of $50,000 with inflation adjustments. Does it still end up at the same amount? Hardly.

BACKWARD

YEAR	HYPOTHETICAL PORTFOLIO RETURN	WITHDRAWAL	END OF THE YEAR BALANCE
INITIAL BALANCE: $1,000,000			
1989	-36.55%	$50,000	$602,775
1990	5.48%	$51,500	$581,484
1991	15.61%	$53,045	$610,929
1992	4.83%	$54,636	$583,161
1993	10.74%	$56,275	$583,474
1994	28.36%	$57,963	$674,545
1995	-21.97%	$59,702	$479761
1996	-11.85%	$61,493	$368,703
1997	-9.03%	$63,338	$277,790
1998	20.89%	$65,238	$256,953
1999	28.34%	$67,195	$243,535
2000	33.10%	$69,211	$232,024
2001	22.68%	$71,288	$197,191
2002	37.20%	$73,426	$169,805
2003	1.33%	$75,629	$95,428
2004	9.97%	$77,898	$19,278
2005	7.49%	$19,278	$0
2006	30.23%	$0	$0
2007	-3.06%	$0	$0
2008	31.48%	$0	$0
AVERAGE RETURN: 10.26%		TOTAL WITHDRAWAL: $1,027,122	

Do you notice anything peculiar here? The same returns, with the same 10.26 percent average, produce drastically different results the moment withdrawals enter the picture. While one order of returns produced a $2.8 million ending balance, the opposite order bankrupted you after fifteen years.

This illustration brings up a critical point: the first ten to fifteen years of your financial independence are the most important.

If you start strong and build up a headwind, you're in much better shape than if the good years come later in life. If you head in the wrong direction early, you could end up broke.

These are the forces conspiring to keep you from financial independence:

- Pensions and social security are no longer reliable.
- Financial independence is therefore more expensive and your responsibility.
- The lottery of returns you get could make or break you.

One way to insulate yourself from these risks is to bring more money to the table. Retiring with $5 million instead of $1 million greatly decreases the chances you'll run out of money before you die, but that's not a viable option for everyone.

If you need a plan to turn your assets into income that gives you financial independence, start by considering this basic question: How much do I need saved to be financially independent?

THE PRICE TAG OF YOUR FINANCIAL INDEPENDENCE

Many of our clients have two primary concerns regarding income planning:

1. They don't know their "number," or how much savings they need.
2. They're afraid to spend their savings too fast or too slow.

Both concerns are totally understandable. Unlike buying a loaf of bread, financial independence doesn't come with an easy-to-read price tag. It's a gradually consumed item that you're paying for over an unknown number of years. The unknown element of this equation introduces complexity and causes concern. What happens if you spend too fast and run out of money, or spend too slow and miss out on great opportunities?

These fears can be alleviated with proper planning, a process that begins with putting a price tag on your financial independence. There are too many variables to accurately calculate your number in these pages or fully explain that process to you, so we'll use a demonstration to begin this discussion.

Let's assume you and your spouse are sixty-five and need $70,000 of annual income to be financially independent. Let's suppose you have consistent income from two sources: $30,000 from social security and $10,000 from some rental property. With $40,000 coming from stable sources, you need to cover the $30,000 shortfall from your own savings in order to meet your income needs.

Here are the ground rules:

1. We want to create $30,000 per year for life (with 2 percent increases annually for inflation).
2. We want to solve this goal for the lowest possible price.
3. We want to solve this goal with the highest probability of success.

Knowing one of you will likely live another thirty years, let's start with a simple question. Do you think $50,000 would be enough to cover these $30,000 annual withdrawals throughout the rest of your life? I hope you answered, "No way." Even with a little bit of interest earnings, you'd run out of money in about two years.

Now for a second guess: Do you think $50 million would

be enough? Probably so. Your $30,000 annual withdrawals aren't likely to bankrupt that plan.

Now we are getting somewhere. We know the price tag of your financial independence is somewhere between $50,000 and $50 million. Let's narrow down that range to something more meaningful.

TESTING THE CONVENTIONAL WISDOM

To start, let's examine some of the "conventional wisdom" out there.

Dave Ramsey is a leading financial expert with a nationwide following. In a blog piece titled "How to Wreck Your Nest Egg at Retirement" (which you can read at LifePerfected.com/book), he says the best way to structure your retirement plan is to put 100 percent of your savings into an S&P 500 Index fund and withdraw 8 percent per year, plus 4 percent inflation. The math says you'll need $375,000 to make this plan work ($30,000 divided by 8 percent).

How do we test Ramsey's advice? It's simple. We need to simulate his strategy in a variety of different scenarios. For this example, let's pick three random years: 1980, 1990, and 2000. We will simulate your retirement in each of those years and see how the plan works.

DAVE RAMSEY
ADVICE SIMULATION #1

Annual Income: $30,000	Strategy: 100% S&P 500 Index Fund
Inflation: 4%	Starting Year: 1980

INITIAL BALANCE: $375,000

YEAR	RETURN	WITHDRAWAL	ENDING BALANCE
1980	31.74%	$30,000	$454,487
1981	-4.70%	$31,200	$403,382
1982	20.42%	$32,448	$446,675
1983	22.34%	$33,746	$505,166
1984	6.15%	$35,096	$498,961
1985	31.24%	$36,500	$606,912
1986	18.49%	$37,960	$674,178
1987	5.81%	$39,478	$671,594
1988	16.54%	$41,057	$734,810
1989	31.48%	$42,699	$909,953
1990	-3.06%	$44,407	$839,022
1991	30.23%	$46,184	$1,032,552
1992	7.49%	$48,031	$1,058,298
1993	9.97%	$49,952	$1,108,848
1994	1.33%	$51,950	$1,070,911
1995	37.20%	$54,028	$1,395,115
1996	22.68%	$56,189	$1,642,606
1997	33.10%	$58,437	$2,108,587
1998	28.34%	$60,774	$2,628,121
1999	20.89%	$63,205	$3,100,607
2000	-9.03%	$65,734	$2,760,769
2001	-11.85%	$68,363	$2,373,363
2002	-21.97%	$71,098	$1,796,548
2003	28.36%	$73,941	$2,211,066
2004	10.74%	$76,899	$2,363,436
2005	4.83%	$79,975	$2,393,854
2006	15.61%	$83,174	$2,671,436
2007	5.48%	$86,501	$2,726,712
2008	-36.55%	$89,961	$1,672,957
2009	25.94%	$93,560	$1,989,017
2010	14.82%	$97,302	$2,172,088

The first simulation is a massive success. Not only does your income last for thirty years, but your original $375,000 grows to more than $2.1 million. Result: PASS!

DAVE RAMSEY
ADVICE SIMULATION #2

Annual Income: $30,000	Strategy: 100% S&P 500 Index Fund
Inflation: 4%	Starting Year: 1990

INITIAL BALANCE: $375,000

YEAR	RETURN	WITHDRAWAL	ENDING BALANCE
1990	-3.06%	$30,000	$334,428
1991	30.23%	$31,200	$394,908
1992	7.49%	$32,448	$389,622
1993	9.97%	$33,746	$391,346
1994	1.33%	$35,096	$360,974
1995	37.20%	$36,500	$445,163
1996	22.68%	$37,960	$499,562
1997	33.10%	$39,478	$612,388
1998	28.34%	$41,057	$733,235
1999	20.89%	$42,699	$834,756
2000	-9.03%	$44,407	$718,966
2001	-11.85%	$46,184	$593,059
2002	-21.97%	$48,031	$425,307
2003	28.36%	$49,952	$481,790
2004	10.74%	$51,950	$476,016
2005	4.83%	$54,028	$442,389
2006	15.61%	$56,189	$446,495
2007	5.48%	$58,437	$409,342
2008	-36.55%	$60,774	$221,158
2009	25.94%	$63,205	$198,918
2010	14.82%	$65,734	$152,923
2011	2.10%	$68,363	$86,334
2012	15.89%	$71,098	$17,658
2013	32.15%	$17,658	-
2014	13.52%	-	-
2015	1.36%	-	-
2016	11.74%	-	-

This simulation gets off to a good start but begins to decline after the first decade, eventually going broke in year twenty-two. Result: FAIL!

DAVE RAMSEY
ADVICE SIMULATION #3

Annual Income: $30,000 Inflation: 4%	Strategy: 100% S&P 500 Index Fund Starting Year: 2000

INITIAL BALANCE: $375,000

YEAR	RETURN	WITHDRAWAL	ENDING BALANCE
2000	-9.03%	$30,000	$313,840
2001	-11.85%	$31,200	$249,148
2002	-21.97%	$32,448	$169,100
2003	28.36%	$33,746	$173,734
2004	10.74%	$35,096	$153,532
2005	4.83%	$36,500	$122,691
2006	15.61%	$37,960	$97,960
2007	5.48%	$39,478	$61,689
2008	-36.55%	$41,057	$13,091
2009	25.94%	$13,091	-
2010	14.82%	-	-
2011	2.10%	-	-
2012	15.89%	-	-
2013	32.15%	-	-
2014	13.52%	-	-
2015	1.36%	-	-
2016	11.74%	-	-

The final simulation suffers from the get-go. Dealing with two market downturns, you go broke just nine years into retirement. Result: FAIL!

Do you see how selective time frames can be used to artificially validate bad advice? That's why you must run thousands of simulations in order to prove the reliability of an idea. As you can imagine, it could take quite a while to run all these calculations manually. Luckily, we have institutional financial engines that can perform ten thousand simulations in a matter of minutes. Running the numbers, we find that the Ramsey retirement solution works only 4 percent of the time.

Let's put Ramsey's strategy on the board to see how it compares to other strategies.

STRATEGY	FINANCIAL INDEPENDENCE PRICE TAG	SUCCESS RATE
Dave Ramsey Method	$375,000	4%

Next, let's consider the strategy used by many financial planners, the 4 percent rule.

This planning rule comes from a 1993 study by the Financial Planning Association. A team of financial scientists led by an advisor named Bill Bengen determined that a 4 percent beginning withdrawal rate (indexed for inflation) gave you a failure rate of just 7 percent.

Using this strategy, you would need $750,000 to have a lifetime of secure income ($30,000 divided by 4 percent).

However, in recent years, large investment firms such as Schwab and Vanguard, as well as research organizations such as Morningstar revisited the 4 percent rule and found two major flaws:

1. The original 4 percent rule never considered fees, which are impossible to avoid.
2. Data should be weighted toward current known financial factors—for example, lower interest rates and higher market valuations.

Using this new information, the 4 percent rule now has only a 44 percent success rate under ten thousand simulations.

FINANCIAL INDEPENDENCE		
STRATEGY	PRICE TAG	SUCCESS RATE
Dave Ramsey Method	$375,000	4%
The 4% Rule	$750,000	44%

Pretend you just boarded a plane in New York bound for Paris. The pilot comes over the intercom and says, "Welcome aboard, folks. We have a beautiful day for flying and a 56 percent chance of crash landing in the Atlantic.

Sit back and enjoy the flight." Are you staying aboard, or do you want off that plane? My guess is you would try to find another flight.

In a report published by Morningstar, in order to get your success rate up above 90 percent, the 4 percent rule has been replaced with the 2.8 percent rule. This means that to receive the same $30,000 of reliable lifetime income, you should set aside $1,072,000. Peace of mind is getting more expensive.

Let's look at our updated chart given the findings of the Morningstar report.

STRATEGY	FINANCIAL INDEPENDENCE PRICE TAG	SUCCESS RATE
Dave Ramsey Method	$375,000	4%
The 4% Rule	$750,000	44%
The 2.8% Rule	$1,072,000	90%

If you've listened to experts such as Ramsey or followed the 4 percent rule on the advice of your local financial planner, seeing these numbers might be devastating.

It's not as bad as you think. There is a powerful but seldom-used strategy we would like to introduce called income insurance.

(The studies by the Financial Planning Association and Morningstar are available for your review at LifePerfected. com/book.)

UTILIZING INCOME INSURANCE

Disclaimer: If you're reading this in bed, you might want to sit up. What we're about to discuss is an integral part of our old-fashioned approach to building wealth.

Income insurance (i.e., annuities) gets a bad rap from the financial media because so many of them are terrible products lined with hidden fees. We prefer to think of these products as vehicles, and like the ones we drive, there are many types—good and bad.

The income insurance we recommend to our clients is used to insure you receive a certain annual income even if you run out of money in your account.

You could utilize income insurance to receive the $30,000 annual shortfall we discussed earlier. Unlike Ramsey's plan and the 4 percent rule, this route comes with a guarantee* to last for the rest of your life.

RYAN HEATH

Early in my career, I bought the hype that retirement insurance was awful. That changed one day when I had lunch with a wealthy entrepreneur who was one of my mentors. I was giving the popular "annuities are the spawn of Satan" speech when he cut me off and said, "Did you know all the income I live on comes from annuities I purchased?" I stuttered a bit trying to figure out what to say and wished I could shove the words back into my mouth.

He told me that having insurance on his income gave him the security he needed to take risks in other areas, and although he's not required to have insurance on the four homes he owns—which are worth $12 million—he would never consider going without it. When I asked him why, he said something that's stuck with me to this day.

"You always insure what you can't afford to lose, and no one can afford to lose their income."

*By guarantee, we mean, "All guarantees are based on the claims-paying ability of the underlying insurance company." So it's important to understand the strength of the company you choose.

Right now, you're probably asking the same question our clients ask us: "What do the insurance companies require for income insurance?"

Insurance companies require two things:

- An annual fee to maintain the account, usually between 0.50 percent and 1.25 percent annually
- The requirement to fund the account with a minimum starting balance based on several factors, such as your age and desired income

Using our example, how much would they require for a sixty-five-year-old couple to receive $30,000 of income for the rest of their lives? As of this writing, it would be approximately $725,000.

"What does it mean to have income insurance?" you ask. It means that if the account runs out of money before you die, the insurance company has to keep paying you income. On the contrary, if you pass away with money still in your account, you can leave the remaining balance to the beneficiaries of your choice.

STRATEGY	FINANCIAL INDEPENDENCE PRICE TAG	SUCCESS RATE
Dave Ramsey Method	$375,000	4%
The 4% Rule	$750,000	44%
The 2.8% Rule	$1,072,000	90%
Income Insurance	$725,000	Guaranteed*

With income insurance, you don't have to worry about the lottery of returns.

We often recommend these vehicles as a means of providing ongoing income because they combine a low price tag and a high success rate. The remaining savings can then be invested into higher growth opportunities such as stocks and real estate.

We aren't the only ones who recommend this strategy—many leading researchers suggest it as well. Richard Thaler, a professor of behavioral science and economics at the University of Chicago Booth School of Business, coined the term the *annuity puzzle* as he pondered why more people don't take advantage of this superior strategy.

Knowing that you're guaranteed a certain income also gives you flexibility while you're living your Life.Perfected. If you accumulate $2 million in savings and investments but don't utilize insurance, you have to keep that money on standby if you want to feel secure. That's when the fear of spending too fast or too slow creeps into your mind.

You can't drop $100,000 on a boat without worrying if that choice will come back to haunt you. But if you saved $2 million and used $725,000 on income insurance, you'd be free to spend the extra $1,275,000 knowing you had secure income coming in each month.

Of course, income planning is just one topic. Our next topic is an exciting but often misunderstood part of creating wealth—investing.

INVESTING

*The quickest way to double your money is to
fold it over and put it back in your pocket.*

WILL ROGERS

Many of the preconceived notions you have about investing are probably wrong.

It's not your fault, though. You've been swayed by Holly-
wood blockbusters, the fake financial media (to borrow a
Trumpism), and the exciting stories from friends about hot
stocks and big returns that fail to paint the whole picture.
These factors and more give the impression that successful
investing is highs and lows, with constant excitement.

In reality, successful investing is usually boring and
predictable.

Boring and predictable can yield big results, though.

Many of us have heard the old story that illustrates the power of compounding. It asks a question with a seemingly obvious answer: Would you rather have a penny that doubles every day for thirty days or $1 million? The right answer will likely surprise you.

MAGIC PENNY

	VALUE	
1	$0.01	x2
2	$0.02	
3	$0.04	
4	$0.08	
5	$0.16	
6	$0.32	
7	$0.64	
8	$1.28	
9	$2.56	
10	$5.12	
11	$10.24	
12	$20.48	
13	$40.96	
14	$81.92	
15	$163.84	
16	$327.68	
17	$655.36	
18	$1,310.72	
19	$2,621.44	
20	$5,242.88	
21	$10,485.76	
22	$20,971.52	
23	$41,943.04	
24	$83,886.08	
25	$167,772.16	
26	$335,544.32	
27	$671,088.64	
28	$1,342,177.28	
29	$2,684,354.56	
30	$5,368,709.12	

You might have seen the penny as an ugly duckling without knowing it had the power to transform into a $5.37 million swan. It's the boring and predictable path, in other words.

In the next chapter, we'll look at taxes and what happens to that $5.37 million when you slice away 30 percent of the money after each day. The difference will blow your mind.

Advisors are constantly dispelling the myths that lead so many investors astray. Our clients usually come to us believing there are only a few ways to get rich investing:

1. Buy the right stock ahead of its time and get rich off the growth and dividends.
2. Ride the coattails of a magical money manager who has all the answers.
3. Use complex, high-speed trading algorithms to perfectly time the market.

A 1986 study published in the *Financial Analysts Journal* showed that when it comes to investing, 9 percent of long-term success comes from specific stock selection and only 1 percent comes from timing the market. (You can review this article at LifePerfected.com/book.)

As advisors, we study patterns to find the prudent, most predictable paths to success in whatever area of wealth accumulation our clients need. The prudent, predictable path to investing success comes from asset allocation, a term that was coined by Nobel Prize winner Harry Markowitz in the 1950s. As Markowitz explained, success was most likely when assets were allocated among various classes: macrolevel stocks and bonds, stocks of various size companies, international and emerging market stocks, and so forth.

Because there is no foolproof path to successful investing, asset allocation allows you to move steadily down the middle of the most prudent path. You'll have some winners and losers, but you're unlikely to swing wildly from top to bottom along the way.

Stability is important less for the results you get and more for the effect it has on your emotions, which are the driver of your decisions. The more volatile your returns are, the more volatile your emotions will be. Going from the best year ever to the worst, for example, you're more likely as an investor to bail out and miss the right moments.

THE RIGHT MOMENTS ARE UNPREDICTABLE

The right moments, by the way, occur unexpectedly and in small numbers. Take a look at this chart that shows the market returns over a thirty-year period:

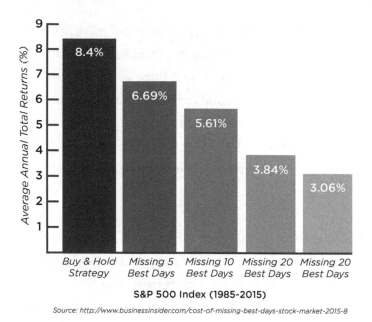

Average Annual Total Returns (%)

Buy & Hold Strategy: 8.4%
Missing 5 Best Days: 6.69%
Missing 10 Best Days: 5.61%
Missing 20 Best Days: 3.84%
Missing 20 Best Days: 3.06%

S&P 500 Index (1985-2015)

Source: http://www.businessinsider.com/cost-of-missing-best-days-stock-market-2015-8

The market earned 8.4 percent on average during this time frame.

If you would've missed the ten best days of those years, you'd have earned just 5.61 percent.

If you would've missed the best twenty-five days, you would've earned only 3.06 percent.

Year-by-year returns are also incredibly hard to predict. Visit LifePerfected.com/book to see a chart listing the year-by-year returns of thirteen asset classes from 1997 to 2016. It perfectly illustrates how snap judgments can affect your portfolio value.

When your emotions dictate your decisions, you can miss the right days or the right years, which can derail your entire investing plan. The way to minimize the effect your emotions have is to walk the boring, predictable path and avoid the big highs and lows.

To use a baseball analogy, successful investors look to hit singles and doubles, not home runs. Some investors need the rush that comes from picking a hot stock or getting a big return. Like hitting a home run, the rush when a risky investment pays off is incredible.

Baseball legend Reggie Jackson knew that feeling all too well, having clobbered 563 home runs during his twenty-one-year career. But did you know that Mr. October also holds the record for most career strikeouts in MLB history with 2,597? That's roughly four and a half strikeouts for every home run Jackson hit during his legendary baseball career.

When it comes to your money, do you want to strike out four and a half times more than you hit it out of the park?

KEEP MISTAKES AND LOSSES TO A MINIMUM

We've found that many people don't understand the math behind losses and how difficult it is to recover from them. If they did, we'd never have to advise a client about minimizing loss again.

A common misconception people have is that if you lose 50 percent in your portfolio in a year, then you need a 50 percent positive return in your portfolio to get your money back.

The math actually reveals a much larger challenge.

If you invest $1 and you lose 50 percent, you have 50 cents. Matching that 50 percent loss with a 50 percent gain leaves you with a 25-cent loss. As this chart shows, you now need a 100 percent return on that 50 cents to get back to your original $1 investment.

THE IMPACT OF LOSSES

STARTING BALANCE: $100,000		
LOSS	END BALANCE	REQUIRED RETURN TO RECAPTURE
-10%	$90,000	+ 11% ⟶ $100,000
-20%	$80,000	+ 25% ⟶ $100,000
-30%	$70,000	+ 43% ⟶ $100,000
-40%	$60,000	+ 67% ⟶ $100,000
-50%	$50,000	+ 100% ⟶ $100,000
-60%	$40,000	+ 150% ⟶ $100,000
-70%	$30,000	+ 233% ⟶ $100,000
-80%	$20,000	+ 400% ⟶ $100,000
-90%	$10,000	+ 900% ⟶ $100,000

This is why we advise our clients to chase only home runs with an amount of money they can totally afford to lose because that is a possible outcome.

For example, if a couple saved $1 million for financial independence and needed only $800,000 to meet their income goals, they could potentially chase a risky investment with the extra $200,000 if they so desired. Any losses on that investment wouldn't eat into their grocery money.

With all the shady investment deals floating around out there, we also have to remind our clients that if it sounds too good to be true, it probably is. As the ancient proverb reminds us, "A fool and his money are soon parted."

A married couple who are clients of ours were reminded of this harsh truth a few years ago when they got swept up with an investment broker in an "opportunity" that made some very lofty claims. We did some due diligence and tried our best to strongly warn them, but they felt good about it and invested six figures. Thankfully, they didn't put their grocery money at risk because the "investment" they were so high on didn't pan out and cost them a lot of money.

Shady investment schemes lure people in because they're desperate for a "magic bullet" that's going to make them rich. We feel that there are no shortcuts to long-term wealth that don't involve a lot of luck (e.g., winning the Powerball). The exact circumstances that aligned to create the overnight millionaires you read about have an astronomically small chance of coming together for you.

As advisors, we act based on financial science, not financial science fiction. As someone looking to build long-term wealth, we recommend you take the same approach.

HOW MUCH RISK CAN YOU HANDLE?

Now that you understand what successful investing looks like and why you must avoid big losses, we can begin the discussion of designing an investment portfolio.

Starting this discussion with clients usually means wading through a mess of disparate accounts, brokers and advisors who never communicated, and hidden fees galore. To simplify things, we look at old and new investments with two questions in mind:

1. How much potential opportunity do we think exists?
2. How much volatility (or movement) will we have to put up with to get that potential opportunity?

These two questions are your starting point regardless of the investment.

A certificate of deposit (CD), as of this writing, has around 1 percent to 2 percent of annual interest earning opportunity with zero volatility or movement. A real estate investment or a corporate stock, on the other hand, is unknown on both fronts. The opportunity depends on the story you're being told and whether you believe it. Volatility predictions, while not a perfect science, are far more predictable.

In our industry, most advisors begin by asking clients their desired return. If the client says 10 percent, the advisor builds a portfolio of assets with a track record of earning 10 percent.

There are two glaring reasons why this logic is backward:

1. Past performance is not an indicator of future results (we try to make the financial regulators happy by saying this as often as we can), so putting together a portfolio that *should* do well because it *has* done well is a false premise.
2. Studies show that your ability to handle volatility is the primary predictor of long-term results, regardless of how the investment actually performs.

Determining how much volatility you can handle is the first question we ask every client, and as you might guess, we want a quantifiable number.

That number is your maximum drawdown. Let's look at how you calculate it.

DETERMINING MAXIMUM DRAWDOWN

In October 2007, the S&P 500 stock market index began the decline that would become the Great Recession. There were days the market would rebound and give everyone false hope, but the slide continued until March 2009 when the market hit rock bottom.

In those seventeen months, the index declined 53 percent. That number was the maximum drawdown for this period—the decline percentage from peak to trough.

Investors such as Warren Buffett were able to stomach a maximum drawdown that high because they saw everything on sale and purchased assets for cheap. For many investors, dealing with a 53 percent drop would've caused them to develop ulcers.

We don't expect that most people have a Buffett-level tolerance for risk, but if you want to invest, your maximum drawdown can't be 0 percent. If that's the case, your only path forward is loading up on CDs or other fixed-rate, guaranteed investments. Virtually all investing requires risk, but we do have some control over that variable.

The variable that advisors can't control is return, which is why we seldom start our conversations talking about this subject. We have never been able to understand why advisors make promises they can't keep and then send you a statement every month to prove they were wrong.

What we can do is start with something like a 10 percent

maximum drawdown and build a portfolio that is highly unlikely to break that threshold. From there, you'll get whatever returns come your way, but you won't be sweating bullets the entire time. Peace of mind is worth a lot too.

Of course, we'd never ask you to pull a number out of thin air. We want you to know for certain what your maximum drawdown is, which is why we've designed our Volatility Profile Quiz to help you know exactly how much risk you can handle.

Visit LifePerfected.com/book to take the quiz.

The Volatility Profile Quiz was built on behavioral finance logic. This is an indispensable tool for investment planning as the questions help you discover your true feelings toward risk and volatility.

Whatever score you get, build your portfolio around that number, not your desired return.

Now comes the fun part—deciding what assets to add to your investment portfolio.

INVESTING AS AN OWNER OR A LENDER

In the investing world, there are owners and there are lenders.

Owners look at an investment and see a story that contains the hope of gain. But in order to achieve that gain, owners must stomach some uncertainty along the way.

Lenders are looking for certainty. They can accept a smaller return in exchange for a promise from the borrower of what is going to happen and what they'll get in the end.

The results of your Volatility Profile Quiz indicate your recommended mixture of owner and lender investments.

Stocks are a popular option for owner investors. *Stock* is a generic term for a piece of ownership in a business entity. If you bought stock in Exxon, you'd become an owner of a tiny sliver of that company. Assuming Exxon did well, the value you'd receive on that investment would come through increased stock prices and dividends.

On the other hand, if Exxon performs poorly or gets edged out by the competition, your investment might not pan out the way you believed it would when you bought into the story. That's the risk you run as an owner buying stock in a public company.

If stocks are for owners, then bonds are for lenders. Sticking with our previous example, if Exxon needed to borrow $100 million to build a new refinery, they could sell bonds that promised to pay bondholders something like 5 percent interest for twenty years before returning the investment in full.

If you bought a bond, you'd be lending Exxon money knowing your rate of return and the time frame after which you'd be fully paid back. With bonds, there's no mystery. Of course, the risk with bonds is that the borrower breaks their promise. For example, if Exxon filed bankruptcy, this could mean a default on their bond obligations that leaves bondholders empty-handed. This is one of the reasons why it's so important to do proper due diligence on all your investment opportunities.

Mutual funds work for both owners and lenders. When you invest in a mutual fund, you're buying a bunch of stocks or bonds packaged together with some kind of theme (e.g., large companies in the oil industry). Mutual funds have a group of managers who decide what to buy and sell, and charge a fee for their services.

THE HIDDEN COSTS OF MUTUAL FUNDS

Depending on which company you invest with and

how many questions you know to ask, you could end up paying a higher fee than someone else for the same mutual fund.

Think about it like a buying a bottle of Budweiser—you'll pay $1 at the grocery store, $6 at the ballpark, and $10 at the Ritz-Carlton. It's the same beer, but the cost is based on what the market will bear. The Ritz knows you'll pay ten times more than you would at the grocery store for the same beer when you're relaxing at their pool.

For the seasoned investor who knows how to access the market, a mutual fund company might charge a 0.25 percent fee. But for the newbie who walks in off the street and doesn't know what to ask, the company might charge a 2 percent fee for the same mutual fund.

The mutual fund industry depends on a lack of transparency with its fees. Because fees are peeled off the fund from behind the scenes, most people don't even realize what they're paying.

A good advisor should be able to examine your portfolio and tell you exactly how much you're paying in fees. If you don't yet have an advisor, you can use the Fee X-Ray Tool on our website, LifePerfected.com/book, to see what your portfolio is costing you.

Another "secret" of the industry is the pay-to-play system that prioritizes the highest bidders on preferred provider lists (i.e., marketing, not merit) and rewards brokers and financial advisors with kickbacks for selling funds to customers at inflated prices.

RYAN HEATH

I spent my first three years in the financial services industry as an advisor and low-level manager before being selected to serve as division manager for a large, publicly traded investment firm. My new role gave me access to corporate management meetings that had previously been above my pay grade.

We focused a lot in those early meetings on driving up RSBs. I had no clue what this acronym stood for, and to avoid looking naïve, I merely nodded along in agreement. After a few months in the dark, I finally pulled a colleague aside and asked him what RSBs were. "Those are revenue sharing bonuses," he told me. "You know, the bonuses the company gets for selling those funds on the preferred provider list."

That's when I discovered that much of the advice promoted by large national investment firms is more profit based instead of merit based.

Kickbacks wouldn't play well in the marketing materials, so the term *revenue sharing* is used to describe these payments. We won't call out any companies, but if you search the web with any large investment company's name plus "revenue sharing disclosure," you can see the insane amounts of money changing hands. One industry giant made $186.7 million from revenue sharing in 2016, or 25 percent of their $746.2 million net income.

We share this information not to discourage you from investing in mutual funds but rather to give you all the details needed for an informed decision. Mutual funds are a convenient option for owners and lenders because they can be stock or bond funds. In fact, most people don't buy stocks or bonds directly but rather through mutual funds.

As long as you know the fees, mutual funds are an appealing option because you have a team of managers working on your behalf. But you're also in an industry where many people are eagerly trying to separate you from your money, so you must be careful.

CONSIDER USING A FIDUCIARY

The financial services industry comes with many different titles—broker, agent, advisor, planner—but if you need help with your investments, you should seek the services of a fiduciary. We operate by the fiduciary standard, which includes standards such as:

- We cannot accept commission from the sale of investment products.
- We do not accept revenue sharing payments (these are additional commissions that some brokers take under the table for pushing specific products).
- We have an obligation to represent our client above all other interests, which includes disclosing any conflicts of interest that may exist.

There are way more stipulations and standards than we care to list here, but the main point is that a fiduciary is working for you and with you. Fiduciaries have fewer conflicts of interest and don't work behind your back to make more money for themselves. Pick up Tony Robbins's book, *Money: Master the Game*, if you want to read more about the fiduciary standard, as Robbins is a huge proponent of using fiduciaries.

DON'T RELY TOO HEAVILY ON INVESTMENTS

No matter how you structure your portfolio or what kind of advisor you choose to work with, we want to make one point very clear—don't rely too heavily on investments.

Despite the hype, investing is not as important as people like to think. Sure, it can help contribute to your long-term financial success, but it's simply one piece of the puzzle. When creating an income strategy, you shouldn't overemphasize investing at the expense of a less "sexy" tactic such as minimizing the tax drain.

With investing, you're along for the ride in the "capitalist sidecar" as the market does whatever it's going to do. In making up for losses and saving for financial independence, you can't depend on results beyond your control. Of course, nothing is ever 100 percent within our control, but we want to tilt the odds in our favor.

When you try to control things that are beyond your control, you become desperate and your decision making suffers. Desperate people jump in and out of investments at the wrong time and fall for schemes that are destined to fail because their emotions are out of control. The best way to avoid this pitfall is to maintain a proper perspective on investing and prioritize a well-rounded approach to income planning.

FOLLOW THE PRUDENT PATH

The prudent path is asset allocation, emotional control, and discipline. It's not sexy, but it's smart.

Sexy options are rarely smart. Did you know a lot of the investment systems in today's market are based on back-tested models? If you dig into the disclosures of a money manager claiming an amazing track record over the past decade, you're likely to find a well-disguised secret: he didn't manage money the past ten years.

Instead, he has a model that "would have" yielded the results he claims had he applied the buy and sell signals at the appropriate times. He's playing Monday morning quarterback with a model that performed favorably after the fact, which is meaningless. The worst part is, he's not alone. Backtesting is not only legal in the investment world, but it's also common practice.

We think the whole system is absurd and a terrible basis on which to make decisions.

Stick to the prudent path and avoid the glare coming off the shiny objects the investment world has to offer. Decide how much risk you can handle and build a diversified portfolio around that number so you can keep your emotions in check.

Building wealth is simple, but it's not easy. You know what is simple and easy? Saving more of your own money rather than worrying about return on investment. With a sound tax strategy in place, you can put more of your money to work for you.

TAXES

*The best way to teach your kids about taxes
is by eating 30 percent of their ice cream.*

BILL MURRAY

Remember the penny that doubled every day for thirty days and became $5.37 million? If not, here's the chart again showing the power of compound interest.

MAGIC PENNY

STARTING VALUE: 1 PENNY
Double balance every day for 30 days.

	VALUE	
1	$0.01	x2
2	$0.02	
3	$0.04	
4	$0.08	
5	$0.16	
6	$0.32	
7	$0.64	
8	$1.28	
9	$2.56	
10	$5.12	
11	$10.24	
12	$20.48	
13	$40.96	
14	$81.92	
15	$163.84	
16	$327.68	
17	$655.36	
18	$1,310.72	
19	$2,621.44	
20	$5,242.88	
21	$10,485.76	
22	$20,971.52	
23	$41,943.04	
24	$83,886.08	
25	$167,772.16	
26	$335,544.32	
27	$671,088.64	
28	$1,342,177.28	
29	$2,684,354.56	
30	$5,368,709.12	

If you scraped off 30 percent of tax each day, what do you think your new total would be?

Surely it'd be at least $1 million...right?

Wrong. At the end of thirty days, you'd have just $48,136.

If the story in chapter 4 illustrates the power of compounding, this story illustrates the way that taxes drain your wealth. Whenever you peel 30 cents off every dollar you make, your money's ability to work for you is weakened. That might not seem like a big deal when you're looking at a dollar, but if it's $1 million and you're left with just $700,000 after taxes, you've lost the ability to create future value with that $300,000.

MAGIC PENNY

	VALUE AFTER TAX	
1	$0.01	x2 (-30% tax)
2	$0.02	
3	$0.03	
4	$0.05	
5	$0.08	
6	$0.14	
7	$0.24	
8	$0.41	
9	$0.70	
10	$1.19	
11	$2.02	
12	$3.43	
13	$5.83	
14	$9.90	
15	$16.84	
16	$28.62	
17	$48.66	
18	$82.72	
19	$140.63	
20	$239.07	
21	$406.42	
22	$690.92	
23	$1,174.56	
24	$1,996.76	
25	$3,394.48	
26	$5,770.63	
27	$9,810.07	
28	$16,677.11	
29	$28,351.09	
30	$48,196.86	

Disclaimer: Numbers are rounded to the nearest cent.

Creating wealth with a tax strategy might seem tedious, but this low-hanging fruit is easy to pick if you take steps to lessen your tax drain.

We're not CPAs, but after twenty-five years advising clients, we can guess you're likely paying more in taxes than the government requires. We covered investing first because it's the fun topic everyone likes to talk about, but tax strategies that save money can actually be more effective.

For example, if you need $20,000 income for financial independence, your first option would be pulling 100 percent of that money from your savings and investments.

But if you have an efficient tax strategy in place and can save $10,000 in taxes, then you would have to pull only $10,000 from your savings and investments for income. This savings, in turn, means you can get by with less return on your investments, which really means that you should be able to lower the volatility of your investments. So not only do smart tax strategies create more wealth, but they also keep you sane.

A simple change in how you receive your income—say, as a profit versus a salary—can dramatically reduce the amount of income tax you pay.

If you run your own business or work as a 1099 earner, you have the power to deduct portions of your income for business expenses such as supplies, tools, technology, and so forth.

You can also utilize an S corporation (or S corp) to reduce your taxes. If you're a sole proprietor making $60,000 a year, you're paying income tax plus social security or self-employment tax on that income, which is currently about 15 percent in addition to ordinary taxes. But if you set up an S corp and receive half your income as salary and the other half as profit, you'll avoid paying social security or self-employment tax on the $30,000 designated as profit.

An S corp that has relatively low operating cost is now saving you $4,500 a year on your taxes.

The federal government would love if we were all W2 employees with limited flexibility in how we receive our income. Assuming you're not boxed in, the first question you should ask a CPA or advisor is if there's a way to restructure your income so that you can take advantage of any provisions that can lower your tax rate.

INVESTMENTS, DISTRIBUTIONS, AND LEGACY PLANNING

In the investment chapter, we discussed how the financial services industry gets rich off retail investors jumping from one investment to another. Not only does this behavior weaken your investments, but it also makes your portfolio inefficient from a tax standpoint.

Having a portfolio that's tax efficient comes down to answering a few questions:

- How are you receiving your earnings?
- Is that income taxable or tax-free?
- If it's taxable, is it the preferred lower tax rate or the full income tax rate?

If you don't know the answers to these questions or have never considered them, you could be taking two steps forward and one step back with your investments. It's nice to get a 10 percent return, but if that return shrinks to 6 percent after taxes, you're missing out.

We've already explained the need to x-ray any investments for fees, and the same is true with taxes. Ask yourself these tax questions when considering an investment:

- What's the tax rate for this investment?

- Is there a way to structure income from the investment so it's tax-free?

Do your research and don't get whisked away by a sales pitch.

Once you achieve financial independence and begin living off income besides wages, you want your distributions to be taxed as little as possible. That could mean utilizing a Roth IRA as a savings vehicle so that all growth and future distributions are tax-free. You could use real estate that has depreciation to give you tax-free income. If used appropriately, life insurance income can be tax-free too.

These are just a few strategies among dozens that help structure your income so it's as tax efficient as possible. That way, for example, if you need $100,000 of annual income, you don't have to take out $140,000 to cover your income plus taxes. If you've implemented the rules of money, you may be able to just take out the $100,000 you need, thus allowing your money to stretch further than it would if your income was inefficient.

If you have assets that are accumulating wealth, you don't have to wait to begin the process of legacy planning. (We'll cover this more in the next chapter.) You can get with an attorney now and start planning, among other things, how taxes will impact your money after you're gone. Almost everyone is familiar with estate tax, and the good news is that there is currently no federal estate tax for couples with an estate under $11 million. The bad news is that any amount above $11 million is taxed at 40 percent.

You hear horror stories about this tax, such as the family of Miami Dolphins owner, Joe Robbie, having to sell the team and the stadium to cover the estate tax after his death. Elvis allegedly died with $10 million and paid $8 million in estate taxes.

Nobody wants to think about estate tax because it involves confronting death, but if you take steps now to address it, this is one of the easiest taxes to minimize or avoid.

CHARITABLE GIVING IS A HUGE ASSET

One mistake we see our clients make is that they start giving charitably only after they've achieved financial independence. Right or wrong, they don't think about helping others until they know their financial future is secure. What they might not realize is that thanks to our tax laws, it's smarter to give while they're still working because the government ends up paying for a lot of their gifts. By waiting, they give up a huge benefit.

For example, say you earn $100,000 annually from wages. The IRS lets you deduct up to 50 percent of your income each year as charitable donations. If you go that route while you're working, you have to pay income tax on only $50,000.

But if financial independence arrives and you need only $50,000 to be secure, then you get to deduct only $25,000 as charitable donations. It's better to start giving charitably while you're living off wages and let the government foot a larger bill.

Much like income, charitable giving can be structured in such a way that it maximizes tax benefits. Mark Zuckerberg, for instance, announced in December 2015 that he plans to donate 99 percent of his Facebook shares (valued at $45 billion) to charity but with a twist. Instead of setting up a charitable trust or a 501(c) trust, he set up his foundation as a limited liability corporation, or LLC. Going this route allowed Zuckerberg tax breaks on money donated to charitable organizations through the foundation, plus gave him greater control over where the money went.

You probably don't have $45 billion to give away, but like Zuckerberg, you can get creative with your charitable giving to maximize the gift and minimize what you pay in taxes. One obvious example is giving to your church. If you give $25,000 annually to your church, you probably just write a check each week for $500. At the end of the year, you get to enjoy a $25,000 deduction, but that's the only benefit you receive.

Instead of giving money, you could consider donating your highest appreciated asset. Say you bought a stock for $10,000 that's now worth $25,000. If you donated that stock to the church, you would get a $25,000 deduction and wash out the $15,000 of gain that was built up in that stock. The church can keep the stock or sell it for cash.

If you liked the stock and wanted to purchase it again, you could take the $25,000 you would have donated to the church and buy the stock at a higher basis.

CHARITABLE REMAINDER TRUST

One final tax avoidance strategy we use with clients is a charitable remainder trust. Here's how it works: Imagine that you bought a piece of property for $100,000 that is now worth $1 million. You want to sell the property but know you'll end up paying $300,000 on the $900,000 gain, which isn't an appealing option. What you could choose to do instead is set up a charitable remainder trust and donate the property to the trust. In doing so, you can pull income—say 5 percent, or $50,000—off that trust for the rest of your life, and the remainder after you die is donated to charity.

Another benefit of a charitable remainder trust is that once you donate the property and it's owned by the trust, you can sell the property and the profits are tax-exempt because charities don't pay income tax. The entire value of the property remains in the trust instead of just $700,000, which means more money for you and your charity.

You might be asking, "What about my heirs? If I go this route, I'm disinheriting them." No worries. If you wanted to leave something for your heirs, you could peel $10,000 off the $50,000 you're getting from the trust and buy a $1 million life insurance policy. (Again, these numbers are for demonstration purposes only.) Buying life insurance allows you to enjoy residual income while also giving to your heirs and to charity.

If you didn't need income from the trust, you could take the $50,000 you're getting and buy a $4 million life insurance policy to give to your heirs. Suddenly, this $1 million property has transformed into a $4 million inheritance by utilizing a charitable remainder trust.

The best part of this scenario is that whatever route you go, the IRS gets cut out. Instead of getting $300,000 in tax revenue from the sale of your property, they get nothing.

Isn't that music to your ears?

If so, we'd advise you to work with tax professionals to create strategies like these that can work for you. The ideas we share are meant to be illustrative and instructive, not comprehensive. You shouldn't use what we've written as a playbook and try to do things on your own. Tax laws and strategies are constantly changing, so you'd be doing yourself a disservice if you didn't seek the advice of experienced professionals.

Don't be penny wise and pound foolish by attempting to do everything yourself. Invest in yourself and your future—when you start saving on your taxes, you'll be glad you did.

Now that we've covered tax strategy, we're ready to dive into the rules of money one final time with legacy planning, or what to do with your accumulated wealth.

LEGACY PLANNING

*Sometimes the poorest man leaves his
children the richest inheritance.*

RUTH E. RENKEL

When you understand and begin to apply the mechanics
of money to build your wealth, what you'll find is that your
life is divided into three phases:

1. Accumulation: Early in life when you're saving, investing, and building assets
2. Distribution: Once you achieve financial independence and begin to distribute dollars and assets to
   create the income you need
3. Legacy: Transferring the remainder of your wealth
   to the people and causes you care about before and
   after your death

We've discovered with our clients that people don't think about the legacy phase because they haven't figured out the distribution phase. They lack a frame of reference to know whether their income needs will be met once they stop working. Not to mention, most people aren't comfortable planning for what happens when they die.

In the previous chapters, we gave you a framework for knowing when you've achieved financial independence, plus the tools you'll need in the accumulation phase to help you reach that point one day. While we can't make the thought of death any less distressing, we hope the discussions we've had so far give you the peace of mind most people lack.

It's tempting to wrap your arms around your wealth and pray it doesn't run out before you die, but we know that's not the best approach to take. If you do the work in the first two phases, you can feel comfortable starting to plan your transfer strategy.

If you don't feel that level of comfort yet, it's OK.

Set this book down and come back to this chapter once you've strategized more yourself or with your team. We're going to discuss the rationale behind legacy planning and get at the reasons *why* you should give, so the advice will be as relevant then as it is now.

But if you're ready to begin, let's start by exploring why you should broaden your view of legacy planning and embrace any creative ideas you have.

YOU NEED PURPOSE BEHIND YOUR PLANNING

We know that when people lack a framework to assess their financial situation, they'll more than likely neglect a meaningful transfer strategy.

Another obstacle many people face with legacy planning is a lack of motivation.

Perhaps it's a generational thing, but many of our older clients want to split their money between their children and leave it at that. Their kids are responsible and will be able to handle the money they receive, so why worry with planning beyond that?

This simple approach misses the point of legacy planning entirely.

If you've committed to a Life.Perfected., you know that life is about more than money. You should therefore use your wealth to enable moments of perfection during your life and after you're gone. Dumping money into the bank accounts of your loved ones might lead to frivolous spending.

Furthermore, legacies aren't created just by writing checks.

Legacies are created through purposeful planning.

The legacy phase should be as well planned and meaningful as the accumulation and distribution phases. Don't be afraid of your creative ideas for how your wealth can make an impact before and after you're gone. As you'll see in a moment, creative strategies are usually more memorable and enjoyable as opposed to generic ones.

To help guide your thinking, let's look at three big questions.

YOUR RELATIONSHIPS AND VALUES MATTER MOST

You might have heard the saying that there are no U-Hauls behind hearses. We can't take our wealth with us, which begs the question, what should we do with it?

One of the saddest fates we can imagine is your loved ones simply getting a check after you die.

Life.Perfected. encourages the transference of wealth while you're alive, not just after you die. You can leave your loved ones a check, but your wealth should also enable experiences that you get to enjoy alongside them.

RYAN HEATH

My wife, Meredith, is probably the most generous person I know. She is constantly doing for others and will bring gifts to people "just because." I joke with her that every time she buys shoes it costs three times as much as everyone else because she often picks out a pair for a couple of her friends. For her, transfer planning takes place every day. She desires to impact the lives of others now and later. I encourage clients to keep that same mindset when thinking of legacy planning. Don't get so caught up in the future gifting strategies that you miss the opportunity to touch someone today.

Knowing that, transfer planning begins with one simple question: What's important to you?

This can be family member specific (my son Joe) or generic (my not-yet-born grandchildren), or any cause or organization that is close to your heart.

Don't be afraid to get creative in answering this question. We have a client who loves working with horses and children with various disabilities. Instead of just donating to causes that support these two groups, her dream is to use her wealth to create a charity that uses horses as therapy for kids in need. How awesome is that?

In honor of his father who died of throat cancer in 1968, Dr. Philips endowed the Philips Institute for Oral and Craniofacial Molecular Biology at his alma mater, Virginia Commonwealth University (VCU). In his speech, Dr. Philips thanked his father for teaching him the value of "commitment, drive, determination, and above all, about the importance of doing things right." He made that gift to VCU as a way to honor all that his father—a man with no great wealth or education—had done for him.

Tony Robbins is another great example. He partnered with Feeding America for the 100 Million Meals Challenge and donated twenty million meals in 2017. Not only that, he helped the organization create a goal of serving one billion meals by 2025.

Robbins grew up in a household where money was always tight. He remembers having to ask his neighbors for food to feed him and his siblings. At age eleven, something happened that sparked this desire to serve one billion meals: a stranger showed up on his doorstep on Thanksgiving Day with enough food to feed his entire family.

Robbins never forgot how that moment impacted his

life, and now, he's using his fortune to impact millions of others. You may not be able to feed millions of people right now, but you probably have the means to feed one person or one family.

The important thing is the heart you give with, not the amount you give.

Once you decide who or what is important to you, the next question is, what's something you can give them that aligns with your values?

Let's say education is one of your core values. You could structure your transfer so that your younger loved ones only receive an inheritance if they attend college. Better yet, you could incentivize the transfer by offering more money if they maintain a certain GPA.

If you're an entrepreneur, you could endow a fund to help loved ones start a business.

We are, after all, talking about legacy planning and how our wealth can create a legacy that outlives us. You should absolutely let your values guide your transfer strategy to ensure that what's important to you lives on after you're gone.

Once you've done that, the final question to consider

is, how can I structure this transfer so that it's best for the recipient?

Ask yourself if the receiving party would be able to handle a lump sum transfer, or whether they'd be better off with a transfer received gradually. For instance, there is no shame in knowing that your grandchildren couldn't handle a lump sum transfer.

The shame would be giving them a lump sum only for them to blow through it and ruin their lives. We've seen it happen before and the results are not pretty.

Be strategic in how you structure transfers to maximize their effectiveness.

The Kennedys provide a great example of how relationships and values should guide your transfer planning. Using a system of trusts and advanced tax strategies, the Kennedy family fund now covers thirty family members and is worth an estimated $1 billion. Money is available for different purposes but comes with conditions that benefit the family collectively.

For example, the trust is set up in part as a private bank that can make loans to the family. Borrowing money from the trust to finance a land deal means paying that money back and producing a report that recaps what was learned. This benefits the person who borrowed the money by making them reflect on their experience, plus it helps the other family members incorporate that wisdom into future experiences.

The Kennedys are obviously a unique institution, but you can transfer your wealth in such a way that it creates an impact beyond the bank accounts of your loved ones.

EXPERIENCES CAN MEAN MORE THAN MONEY

One creative transfer strategy we love is paying for experiences with your family. If your Life.Perfected. involves spending time with family, going this route can result in the most meaningful transference of wealth possible.

RYAN PETERSON

When he was about eighty years old, my grandfather started talking about his estate plans with my mom and aunt, his two children. Like many people, he was worried that he'd run out of money before he died. My mom and aunt walked him through a process similar to the one we've covered in this book and helped him see he had more than enough money to last for the rest of his life.

When he saw that, he told his daughters that his wealth would be split between the two of them when he died. They suggested instead that the money be spent on a family vacation, an idea my grandfather loved. He took my family and my aunt's family (eleven of us total) to Hawaii and paid for the entire trip—airfare, hotel, food, and excursions.

We still talk about that trip thirty years later and enjoy looking at photos when our families get together. Rather than just writing a check for his two children, my grandfather chose to pay for a vacation that gave us these unforgettable, priceless memories. We're all grateful for his choice and that we got to spend that time together.

We share stories like these with our clients to get them thinking about giving to their kids in the most meaningful way possible. Their natural inclination is to split their wealth among their kids when they die, but as we help them realize, their posthumous gift won't mean as much by the time their kids receive it, if they're even moderately successful.

If your kids are utilizing the mechanics of money to build their own wealth, a boost to their bank account might not mean as much as the family memories you could create. Instead of asking yourself how much you can leave your loved ones, ask yourself how you can impact their lives now while that help could still have a big impact.

If creating experiences for your family is something you value, you can continue doing that after you're gone. We've seen clients stipulate that funds from their trust are dispersed only to family members who attend annual family functions, such as a lake trip for July 4th.

We see this as a great way for our clients to instill future generations with their values and keep families together after the heads of the family are gone.

SHARE YOUR WISDOM AND YOUR WEALTH

When someone accumulates enough wealth to need legacy planning, they have wisdom that is just as valuable as their money. We believe it's their responsibility to share that wisdom with the recipients of their gifts. The last thing anyone wants is for that recipient to wind up like one-third of lottery winners—bankrupt with their life in shambles.

Lottery winners run into trouble because they have no experience handling the amount of money they win and no context for making wise decisions. As a result, they squander wealth that seems impossible to squander. Unless they receive guidance, the average person who inherits wealth will feel as lost and confused as those lottery winners.

When asked what advice he would give to lottery winners, billionaire Mark Cuban offered these words that we think apply to anyone who comes into a large sum of money all at once, either through the lottery or an inheritance:

- Hire a tax attorney first.
- If you weren't happy yesterday, you won't be happy tomorrow. It's money, not happiness.
- If you were happy yesterday, you are going to be a lot happier tomorrow. Life gets easier when you don't have to worry about the bills.

- Feel free to help your friends and family some, but always talk to your accountant first. Also, nobody needs $1 million for anything. They don't even need $100,000. Those who ask for that much money aren't your friends.
- You don't become a smart investor when you win the lottery.

Think about it—most people accumulate their wealth over decades because they were disciplined in their savings, kept their expenses in check, and made wise investments. Depending on the age of the recipient and the size of the gift, those who receive money as part of your legacy planning might not have the benefit of decades of experience.

If you care enough about someone to transfer some or all your wealth to them, you owe it to them to provide guidance so they can handle the money they'll one day receive.

Dr. Philips does this by holding family meetings where everyone has input into business and charitable decisions that are being made. He will weigh their input in his ultimate decision making, but getting them involved in this process provides them with invaluable experience either way. Not only are they contributing their input to financial decisions, but they're also seeing how wealth should be used correctly and positively to impact the lives of others.

The important thing is to take steps to insulate your loved ones from the corrupting influence of wealth. Pour your wisdom into them as early as you can so that when the time comes, they feel empowered to make wise decisions with the money they receive.

NOT ALL WEALTH IS FINANCIAL

As you consider what's important to you and plan the "who" and "how" of transferring your wealth, it's crucial to look at the different kinds of wealth you can share.

For people in the accumulation phase or those trying to figure out distribution, financial wealth is the first type that likely comes to mind. While money is important, we know from discussing a life of perfection that dollars and cents aren't everything. There are other types of wealth that, for the people who have them, mean far more than money.

Lee Brower, author of *The Brower Quadrant* and founder of the Empowered Wealth program, identifies four quadrants of assets, or wealth, in his program:

1. Core: family, values, faith, health, and well-being
2. Experience: education, reputation, networks, knowledge, and wisdom

3. Contribution: contributions made to the well-being of others
4. Financial: money, real estate, investments, material possessions

It's fitting that Brower lists financial assets last because, as we mentioned, it's the type of wealth people typically think of first. But after serving thousands of clients as a coach and strategist, Brower understands that flourishing legacies are built when nonmonetary wealth is transferred to future generations. He shares in his book that if forced to choose, truly wealthy individuals would bankrupt their financial quadrant before any of the others.

For those who aren't wealthy, this sounds ludicrous. But as Brower explains, the wealthy know financial assets are the easiest to replace if the other quadrants are intact.

The core, experience, and contribution quadrants can also grow independent of wealth. Assuming your basic needs are met, you can begin giving to charity today even if the donation is small. If a financial contribution isn't possible, you can give your time.

Most importantly, if you have children, talk with them about what you're doing. Let them help pick the charity and discuss what's important about the work that the charity does. Better yet, encourage them to contribute some of their own money from work or even some of their chore or birthday money if they're young. They need help figuring this out while they're young.

RYAN PETERSON

We teach our kids that with any money they receive, they should spend one-third, save one-third, and give one-third to charity.

The first time we talked to our daughter, Hailey, about this, she was six years old. She was apparently so inspired by our conversation that when we went to pick up dinner later that night and were standing at the counter, she put her entire $5 allowance in the tip jar and said she was "giving it to charity."

The cashier laughed as we politely removed the money and realized we probably had to spend a little more time on the topic. Don't worry, we tipped them with our own money!

Knowledge is freely accessible if you're motivated to look for it. You can take classes from MIT, Harvard, and other prestigious universities for free online. You don't need money to call an expert in your industry and acquire wisdom from them. If you're hungry to learn, some of the best coaching in the world comes through internships.

We've already addressed the core assets, those foundational to a Life.Perfected., and understand the ways we can grow this form of wealth as often as possible.

One of the shared beliefs we have that made us want to work together is that if you add value to the world, money will follow. We talked about this belief in the introduction and revisit it now to give you a framework for adding value to the world. We both like Brower's quadrants and look to add wealth in the first three quadrants as often as we can.

It's totally fine to use a different framework, but just remember that financial wealth is the reward you receive when you are great at creating value the world desperately wants. The biggest mistake we see people make during the accumulation phase is chasing financial assets at the expense of those in the other quadrants, thinking that once they have money, then they'll figure everything else out.

Life doesn't work that way. True wealth flows into your life when you invest in the lives, efforts, and experiences of others. These other forms of wealth don't automatically flow in when your bank account is full. In fact, if you wait until you have financial wealth to add to the other areas, you'll probably find you waited too long to try.

Adding wealth in other areas will make you a wiser, kinder,

and more caring individual who's better equipped to handle financial wealth when you receive it.

These quotes offer great reminders of why you should pursue nonfinancial forms of wealth first if you want to achieve Life.Perfected.

Life isn't about leaving something to people; it's leaving something in people.

PETER STROPLE

The idea is not to live forever; it is to create something that will.

ANDY WARHOL

Carve your name on hearts, not on tombstones. A legacy is etched into the minds of others and the stories they share about you.

SHANNON L. ALDER

HANDING OFF YOUR WEALTH

Much like your income needs for financial independence, there are too many factors to consider for us to discuss specific transfer strategies in these pages. If you'd like to see which options best fit your situation, we have transfer planning resources available on our website, including a Wealth Transfer Assessment at LifePerfected.com/book.

We've covered the reasoning behind transferring wealth in this chapter because it's far more important than the specific fund you use or the tax strategies you employ. In our opinion, deciding what's important to you and the values you want to pass on represents 80 percent of transfer planning. The fine details that constitute the other 20 percent come easy once you lay the groundwork and then educate yourself on specific options or consult your team. Invest in a good estate lawyer once you've got your ideas down on paper. Your financial advisor should be using someone who can help you avoid making mistakes.

As we wrap up this chapter, let's review the cornerstones of the legacy phase.

START AS EARLY AS YOU CAN

The first step of transferring financial wealth happens before the legacy phase even begins—determining the income you need for financial independence. No matter your age or your situation, this can be done right away.

Once you've accumulated the wealth needed for the distribution phase, you can begin transfer planning. Starting this process early has some huge benefits:

- We all hope to be of sound mind if we reach age eighty-five, but the decisions that must be made during this phase are easier to make when you're younger.
- As we discussed in the taxes chapter, the government incentivizes charitable giving while you're alive if that's part of your wealth transfer strategy.
- Transferring after death limits the control and flexibility you have with your wealth.
- You can enjoy the benefits of your wealth if you transfer while you're alive, but if you wait until you're eighty-five to start planning, those opportunities might be gone.
- Use strategic life insurance planning to "buy" your funded legacy goals for pennies on the dollar.

Early planning allows you to use your financial wealth to grow assets in other areas, thereby enriching your life and the lives of others while you're around to enjoy it.

TRANSFER YOUR VALUES FIRST

No matter how wealthy you are, your values are the greatest gift you can leave your loved ones.

RYAN PETERSON

My youngest son, Ethan, plays little league baseball, and the parents of some of the other kids on his team are among the most successful winemakers and grape growers in Napa Valley.

These folks grace the covers of wine and travel magazines and have more money than they could ever need, yet they take time to volunteer as coaches, help out at the snack shop, and sell $20 T-shirts to help raise money for the team. They just want to be grounded and teach their kids the importance of giving back to their community.

Are you actively demonstrating your values to your loved ones? Simple acts such as helping the family plan for an annual vacation or volunteering for organizations require no financial assets and speak volumes to your loved ones about what's important to you.

SHARE YOUR WISDOM

You would never give your kids the keys to a Ferrari without first teaching them to drive it safely, so why would you write your kids a check without teaching them how to handle wealth responsibly? As we've seen countless times during our careers with clients and friends, money without an understanding of how to use it can lead to ruin.

Along with your values, the knowledge you acquired accumulating your wealth must be passed down to the recipients of your wealth before the first check is ever written.

RYAN HEATH

I have a client who has handwritten annual letters to everyone in his family for the past thirty years. Each letter is delivered on New Year's Eve and includes a recap of what he learned that year, plus appreciation for that family member and pieces of advice for their life.

These letters cost nothing and require no great talent, but they are immensely meaningful to the recipients. In fact, I bet his family members would say that if their house were on fire, those letters would be one of the first things they grabbed.

We can sometimes overthink the extravagance of our transfer strategy, but the legacy we leave can be as simple as thoughtful words of wisdom.

We're again reminded of Dr. Philips, who has carefully divided his wealth between gifts to his family and gifts to charity because he knows their lives will be enriched more if he shares his nonfinancial wealth. Even today, his daughter works full time looking for worthy causes for their family foundation. Like a member of the Kennedy family, she also must complete a report detailing how each organization benefitted from its gift.

"I want my kids to make society better in their lifetimes and work hard," Dr. Philips told us.

Dr. Philips has worked throughout his life to share his values of hard work and social responsibility with his family. He also teaches them how to avoid squandering their wealth by showing them ways to grow nonfinancial assets critical to a Life.Perfected.

We encourage you to adopt the same mindset as you consider how to transfer your values to future generations and create a legacy that will endure long after you're gone.

TAKE ACTION

Knowing is not enough; we must apply.
Willing is not enough; we must do.

BRUCE LEE

In this book, you've learned about the rules of money and how wealth should enable your Life.Perfected., not define it. Now it's time to act!

Action is the impetus for greatness, as this story reminds us:

Abraham Lincoln was asked by an aide about the church service he had attended. Lincoln responded that the minister was inspired, interesting, well prepared, and eloquent and the topic relevant.

"Then it was a good service?" the aide asked.

"No," Lincoln responded.

The aide protested, "But Mr. President, you said that the minister was inspired, interesting, well prepared, and eloquent and that the topic was relevant."

"Yes," replied Lincoln, "but he didn't challenge us to do any great thing."

We meet so many people who wait for the perfect answer before they'll make a move financially and they end up missing golden opportunities. You'll find moments of perfection if you seek them, but there are no perfect answers when it comes to money.

RYAN HEATH

One of my early mentors always encouraged me to "fail forward." What he meant by that was I should act even when I know failure is the likely outcome because I can use that moment of failure to learn and get better.

He would say that wanting to succeed in life without encountering failure is like wanting to play football without getting tackled. The two go together.

This is an unpredictable arena in which we play. The wisdom we've shared in this book will give you a better chance at long-term success, but the risk of failure is always there.

For some, this fear of failure is crippling. If it can't be perfect, they don't want to try.

As Dan Sullivan at Strategic Coach says, "Focus on progress, not perfection."

He understood that taking steps toward achieving your goal was more valuable than waiting around and doing nothing. Yes, there's a chance you might not ultimately create the wealth you want, but there's a zero percent chance you'll create wealth if you don't act. The perfect path is never coming, so you might as well create your own.

As you take action, don't worry if you feel out of your depth in certain areas—you're in good company. After nearly half a century of combined experience in this industry, we can assure you that everyone struggles in one area of their finances or another.

To help you understand your deficiencies and address them so you can move forward in confidence, let's look at a concept we created called the Wealth Quotient.

THE WEALTH QUOTIENT

In 1916, the Binet-Simon intelligence test became the standard method of measuring a person's intelligence quotient, or IQ. Society's understanding of intelligence has evolved over the past century and we now know that several forms of intelligence exist.

What we never liked about the standard intelligence test was that after you learned your IQ, you weren't instructed on how to improve your intelligence. Whatever score you got was assumed to remain static throughout your life no matter how your intelligence evolved. Finding out you had a low IQ could therefore be demoralizing to your confidence.

In creating a way to measure someone's Wealth Quotient (WQ), we placed a high priority on not only recognizing deficient areas but also providing strategies for improvement.

The Wealth Quotient looks at financial intelligence in three areas: capital, wisdom, and action.

The larger the area of overlap between the circles for capital, wisdom, and action, the greater your WQ. Luckily, the remedy for each area of weakness is straightforward:

The Wealth Quotient

- Capital: While not necessary, it helps to have money in order to make money. If you don't yet have enough, you've got to employ the rules of money to build your wealth over time.
- Wisdom: Again, this book is a great starting point, but if you need more wisdom, you can teach yourself or pay for advice from experts and advisors.
- Action: Einstein famously said, "Nothing happens until something moves," so if you're not moving, you shouldn't expect much.

To read more about the Wealth Quotient and utilize the resources we have available to foster improvement in each area, please visit LifePerfected.com/book.

When we work through the Wealth Quotient with clients and identify areas where they can improve, some of them are hesitant to take action. That's when we have to step in with a gentle reminder that they've hired us to help them improve their situation, and if they're not willing to take the actions we recommend, they've hired the wrong group.

RYAN PETERSON

One of my roles as a financial advisor is to help clients get clear enough about their dreams and goals that they could see them in a mirror if I held it up for them. As we work together, I'll periodically "hold the mirror up" to see if the vision they had is closer or further away from reality.

This allows them to see the positive and negative consequences of their actions and helps us course correct if needed to keep moving toward their objectives. Achieving goals can be hard work, and it's my job to help clients avoid distractions.

You picked up this book because you wanted to learn how to create wealth and enjoy a Life.Perfected. We can tell you without a doubt that we feel a connection exists between people with a high WQ and people who are enjoying an ideal life.

If you're reading this and have identified the area you should focus on to raise your WQ, don't let this realization be your stopping point.

Move forward and take the steps needed to see that score improve.

WEALTH IS CREATED EVERY DAY

Conventional wisdom has long dictated that retirement is that magical date after which your income needs will be met and you can begin enjoying life. We've debunked this notion and replaced it with the idea that life is to be enjoyed every day. It's also helpful to apply the same logic to any magical date we're anticipating:

- Paying off our mortgage or car loan
- Getting a raise at work
- Receiving our tax refund

Once these days arrive, we're convinced we won't have to worry about money as much. The anticipation of them makes us apathetic and inactive, causing us to ignore or lose interest in the habits we should be practicing every day to grow our wealth.

For example, anticipating that raise at work can make us hold off on contributing to our 401(k). Once we have more money, we'll be able to give. If we can't give the perfect amount we think we should be giving, then we'll give nothing.

What would happen if you contributed $5 out of each paycheck instead of waiting?

We can all buy one less cup of coffee to spare $5 per paycheck. While it's true that $5 doesn't make a huge impact on our savings, contributing every time we get paid is an invaluable habit that'll likely lead to larger contributions in the future. Think back to the study on employees who were automatically enrolled in 401(k) plans at work and how 80 percent of them increased their contribution over time.

Small habits can yield big results the longer we practice them.

To discover more habits that make a long-term difference, pick up the *New York Times* best seller *The Automatic Millionaire* by our friend and business partner, David Bach.

You don't have to wait for that magical date when you receive your raise or pay off your loans. Today is as magical a day as any to start practicing good habits.

The vast majority of wealthy people didn't get that way due to "lightning strike" moments such as winning the lottery or receiving an inheritance. The people who built wealth and maintained it long term are those who made small changes throughout their life. After so many years, those small changes reached a tipping point and combined to create a powerful wave of wealth creation. Every small decision they made paid off.

Don't wait for magical dates or lightning-strike moments—they're not the answer.

Take the small steps today you know will help create the wealth you want.

WHAT ARE YOUR ACTION STEPS?

Of course, we're not the type of advisors who pound the table and tell you to take action without telling you what actions you should take. We realize this book has covered a lot of ground and your head might be spinning right now. To help you start moving forward today (not tomorrow or next week), look at these action steps below:

- Define a perfect day in these categories: family, for yourself, career, and charity.
- Create a balance sheet to assess where you stand and begin tracking future growth.
- Use an income statement to review your money in versus money out.
- Take the Volatility Profile Quiz to learn how much risk you can handle.
- Learn more about your Wealth Quotient and how it contributes to your success.

If you need them, we have ten more actions steps on our website, LifePerfected.com/book.

As Lao Tzu once said, "The journey of a thousand miles begins with a single step." We want you to begin your journey by picking two action steps you're going to do today and writing them down.

....

....

The reason we kept the list short (we could've listed twenty-five) and limited you to two action steps is so you don't get overwhelmed with analysis paralysis. Staring at twenty-five items and not knowing where to start or how many to tackle could've locked up your brain and kept you from taking action today. We want to help you focus and avoid brain freeze.

As for which steps to pick, think back on the time you've spent reading this book and recall any light bulb moments you had where the words leaped off the page at you. We're willing to bet there were at least two points along the way where you made mental notes to follow up on once you finished the book. Well, the time has come to follow up!

Would you like some help? If so, reach out to us at LifePerfected.com/contact. We work with clients throughout the United States, and our team would be happy to help in any way possible.

If you know the steps you want to take, write them down and commit to making them happen today. You won't mess up your book by writing in it; we do it all the time! It's one of the best habits we've found for following through with important actions.

Allow us to remind you why action is important with a final look at Life.Perfected.

WEALTH SHOULD SUPPORT LIFE.PERFECTED.

If you take nothing else away from this book, let it be this: **wealth is meant to enable Life.Perfected., not define it.**

If you're chasing a higher number in your bank account so you can buy a bigger house or an expensive car, you'll discover one day that your life is far from perfect. Perfection is found not in the *money* you accumulate but in the *moments* you experience.

Moments of perfection can happen every day in big and small ways. From a late-afternoon walk with your spouse to a family vacation in Hawaii, you have the power to create your perfect life. In the same way wealth is the accumulation of small changes stretched over time, a Life. Perfected. is the accumulation of moments of perfection lived every day.

If you think you need wealth to live this life, you're mistaken. Wealth can fuel your costlier ambitions, but perfection is free and easy to come by if you have the right outlook. To illustrate this point, we have one final story to share with you.

An American investment banker met a local fisherman at the pier of a small coastal village in Mexico. The banker started talking with the fisherman, and when he saw the large yellowfin tuna in the man's boat, he asked how long it took him to catch the fish.

The fisherman responded, "Only a little while." When the banker heard this, he asked why the fisherman didn't stay out longer and catch more fish, to which the fisherman replied that he had enough fish to support his family's immediate needs.

What, then, the banker asked, does the fisherman do with the rest of his day?

"I sleep late, fish a little, play with my children, take siestas with my wife, stroll into the village each evening where I sip wine, and play guitar with my amigos."

The banker scoffed and explained that with his help, the fisherman could launch a full-blown fishing empire that would include a fleet of fishing boats, his own cannery, and a New York office. Within ten years, the fisherman could announce an IPO and make millions.

"After I make millions, then what?" the fisherman asked.

"Then you could retire," the banker said. "Move to a fishing village where you would sleep late, fish a little, play with your kids, take siestas with your wife, stroll into the village in the evenings where you could sip wine and play your guitar with your amigos."

Perfection is not found in chasing a number, nor does it reside in your bank account.

It's found in the sunset strolls, the meals enjoyed with good friends, and the laughter of your children. If you just know where to look, you'll see perfection all around you.

ACKNOWLEDGMENTS

RYAN HEATH

In life, you will realize there is a role for everyone you meet. Some will test you, some will use you, some will love you, and some will teach you. But the ones who are truly important are the ones who bring out the best in you. They are the rare and amazing people who remind you why it's worth it.

—UNKNOWN

To my clients, for your trust—thank you.

To my fellow financial advisors, who allow me to pick your brains and plagiarize your ideas—thank you.

To my mother, Deborah, who always made me think I was smarter than I actually was—thank you.

To my father, Jon, who demonstrated what it truly means to live a life of service to others—thank you.

To my grandfather, Frank Shaw, for helping me set up my first mutual fund account (still the best investment I ever had)—thank you.

To my son, River, whose drive and determination I strive to mimic—thank you.

To my son, Reed, whom I hope to work for one day—thank you.

To my daughter, Finley, whose laugh makes my heart smile—thank you.

Finally, to my wife, Meredith, who endures my constant state of change and fascination with big ideas. You are generous, driven, resilient, selfless, and about ninety-six other words I aspire to be. Your love and support is a constant reminder of what really matters when designing a Life.Perfected. Thank you.

RYAN PETERSON

Someone once told me that you own all of your failures and owe all of your successes. I believe that to be true, and there are a lot of people I owe for helping me go down the right path over the years. I've worked with incredible people, and a few deserve special recognition. Steve Kumagai, who told me that "You either lose great people because you promote them or because you don't promote them; I've always been the former." Marty Pluth, who always invited me into his home and treated me like family from my first day on the job. Penny Mathis, the glue that has held everything together at Copperleaf Capital since its very beginning in 1986, when it was Philips Investments. Dr. John Philips, who's taught me so much as a business partner and friend.

My parents, who I know are proud of me, even though my mom always wanted me to be a choral conductor. My kids: Hailey, who I miss already as she finishes her last year at home. She is incredibly creative and never afraid to be herself. She is a talented singer and actress who I know will continue to do amazing things on- and offstage in college and beyond. Will, my son with a kind heart, a great golf swing, and serious ball-handling skills on the court. He is an amazing role model for his brother and everyone around him. Ethan, who can always make me laugh, surprise me with magic tricks, sink three-pointers from anywhere, and is never ashamed to show off his six-pack abs.

Of all the people who mean so much in my life, the greatest gratitude I have is to my wife, Heather. She served our country as a major in the air force and is one of the finest physicians I've ever known. She's a wonderful mother and spouse, especially with her extensive knowledge of nutrition. (My kids would eat only pizza and omelets if it were up to me!) She's always supported my goals in life, whether they were important or trivial. She's always been there to ground me with charitable work and remind me what's truly important in life. She's been a mentor and my best friend for almost twenty years, and I know the best is yet to come. She becomes more beautiful to me every day. I love you, honey. You make Life.Perfected. for me.

ABOUT THE AUTHORS

RYAN HEATH

Ryan Heath knew from an early age that he wanted to help people in his career. It was that desire that led him to team up with Ryan Peterson in 2015 and form Copperleaf Capital, a firm dedicated to creating and protecting the financial legacies of clients.

Ryan also has a passion for sharing his expertise with others. In addition to being an author, he's also a public speaker, editorial contributor, former radio host, and has served in leadership and board positions for multiple industry associations.

Ryan is currently living his Life.Perfected. in Raleigh, North Carolina, with his wife, Meredith, and their three children—River, Reed, and Finley. They enjoy traveling and tailgating for their favorite college sports team, the LSU Tigers. Whether he's hitting a hole in one or nailing a caddie with a tee shot at Pebble Beach, Ryan will happily take whatever perfect moments he can get on the golf course.

RYAN PETERSON

Ryan Peterson is committed to making a difference in people's lives through his work. At Copperleaf Capital, where he serves as partner with Ryan Heath, he works with clients to help build wealth that serves the pursuit of a better life.

Ryan has been in the financial industry for twenty years as an advisor and six years building financial planning infrastructures for *Fortune* 500 companies. His vision for Copperleaf Capital—helping clients create their Life. Perfected.—came from those years working for large financial companies that didn't always put clients first.

Ryan's Life.Perfected. took him and his wife, Heather, and their children—Hailey, Will, and Ethan—from Ralcigh, North Carolina, to Napa Valley in 2016. His perfect moments include sunrise walks to the bakery with family and wine tastings with Heather. He hopes to run a marathon in all fifty states before age fifty—if his legs don't give out first!